E. E. Brandstaff

ACROSS THE BOUNDARIES
OF ORGANIZATIONS

ACROSS
THE BOUNDARIES
OF ORGANIZATIONS

An Exploratory Study
of Communication Patterns
in Two Penal Institutions

Thomas Mathiesen
Institute for Social Research, Oslo

© 1971 by The Glendessary Press, Inc.
2512 Grove Street, Berkeley, California

Printed in the United States of America
Library of Congress Catalog Card No. 79-119705

CONSULTING EDITOR:

Donald A. Hansen
University of California, Berkeley

CONTENTS

PREFACE

This essay deals with external and internal communication patterns in penal institutions. It is based on intensive interviews in two penal establishments in one of the Scandinavian countries.

To protect the anonymity of those interviewed, the particular institutions and the country in which they are located are not disclosed in the essay. The Scandinavian countries are sufficiently similar in terms of social and cultural background as well as language to make this procedure legitimate.

A first draft of the essay was written while I was visiting assistant professor at the University of California, Santa Barbara. I wish to express my gratitude to the members of the Department of Sociology in that university for helpful and stimulating discussions. I also wish to thank the staff members at the Institute for Social Research, Oslo, for stimulation and support during the completion of the essay, and the staff members in the two penal establishments concerned for their helpfulness and interest in my work.

THOMAS MATHIESEN
Oslo

ACROSS THE BOUNDARIES

OF ORGANIZATIONS

I

PROBLEM

AND RESEARCH

SETTING

Humans never exist in a social void. Even those of us who live isolated from others are related to others—if through nothing else, through isolation itself. For isolation is a definite engagement, as Georg Simmel noted long ago:

> Isolation . . . refers by no means only to the absence of society.
> . . . Isolation attains its unequivocal, positive significance only as
> society's effect at a distance. . . . Isolation is thus a relation. . . .

If this holds for individuals, it is no less true of whole organizations. Relations between organizations are ubiquitous. And relations between organizations affect the organizations internally, not unlike engagements that affect the individual "inside." Isolation of organizations from one another is at times the most jolting kind of relation they can have.

In its most general terms, the sociological concern in this essay is that of how an organization's relationship with its social environment shapes the organization's internal affairs.

This general problem is strategic for organization theory.

Recent decades have seen an upsurge of interest in organizational research. Some of this research treats the organization as an "open system" (see for example Thompson 1962, Udy 1962, Katz and Kahn 1966, Thompson 1967, Yuchtman and Seashore 1967, Gustavsen 1969, Chapter 10) thereby including the possible influence of boundary relations on internal life. But a majority of organizational studies still deal with internal arrangements alone, ignoring the possible impact of external relations. To mention only one example, we know very little about the ways in which organizations are interlinked in complex networks, and about how such networks bear upon processes within the individual organization. In general, organizational behavior which now is explained exclusively in the light of internal arrangements may require drastic reinterpretation when external relations are considered.

But the problem is not important for the theory of organizations only. It is also significant for theory concerning social interaction between individuals. Organizations are related to the social environment in various ways, but in some fashion or other, direct or indirect interaction between individual insiders and outsiders is involved. An organization's relations with the social environment may shape internal affairs in numerous ways, but again interaction between individuals is necessarily involved. Analysis of the problem I have specified may therefore tell us something about the principles of interaction between individuals. In subsequent chapters, I shall discuss implications for interaction theory as well as for the theory or organizations.

I wish to consider some features of the above-mentioned general problem as they may be observed in penal institutions. The sociology of penal establishments is probably the area of organizational research in which the possible impact of external relations on internal life is most grossly ignored.

Though the history of research in such organizations has gone through several phases, the shifts in theoretical interest have hardly at all been paralleled by a widening of the perspective to include external relations.

A brief historical review may show more clearly how research in penal institutions has neglected our problem. The first phase of sociological prison research, before the outbreak of World War II, was primarily represented by one man. Donald Clemmer, the pioneer of prison sociology, published his classical case study *The Prison Community* in 1940 (Clemmer new ed. 1958). The most important part of Clemmer's work consists of his theory of inmate prisonization within the walls. By "prisonization" Clemmer meant the taking on of the deviant values, customs and culture in general of the penitentiary. Through prisonization the inmate presumably takes on a criminalistic ideology, which leaves him fairly immune to influence from conventional norms and values. Clemmer hypothesized a negative association between degree of prisonization and adjustment after release. In a sense, then, he was interested in the relationship between the prison and the external community: the greater the convict's involvement in the inmate culture behind the walls, the poorer his adjustment to the community was expected to be. But Clemmer was apparently not very interested in how the prison's relations with the outside world may shape internal structure and process. (An exception to this is his stress on inmate contacts outside the walls as ameliorating the degree of prisonization on the inside.)

Clemmer's work remained more or less alone in prison literature for a long time. A review of publications after the appearance of his book discloses a dearth for the years during and immediately after World War II, and interest in this field of sociology was not permanently revived before the late fifties. Among the many works that appeared in this second phase of the study of prisons, Gresham M. Sykes' case study

The Society of Captives is particularly well known (Sykes 1958). In this influential book, Sykes dealt with some of the problems discussed by Clemmer, but from a new point of view. Unlike Clemmer he did not emphasize the question of how prisoners take on the deviant subculture of the penitentiary. Rather, he stressed the question of why the presumed culture came into existence in the first place. He looked not for the conditions determining degree of socialization into the deviant culture, but rather for those explaining why the culture arose. In explaining the origin of the deviant inmate culture, Sykes presented a functional theory.[1] He argued that many of the deprivations associated with imprisonment are extremely painful from the point of view of inmates, and that an inmate culture arises as a defensive response to the pains of imprisonment. The inmate subculture, he claimed, stresses the theme of inmate cohesion against the staff and the law-abiding world. Insofar as such a culture of cohesion is institutionalized, the pains of imprisonment are presumably reduced. In discussing his functional theory, Sykes considered only arrangements internal to the prison; he did not consider the possibility that institutional relations with the environment might influence internal life. In other words, whatever the differences between Clemmer's and Sykes' contributions, they are alike in viewing the prison as more or less divorced from the external world. This tendency may be reflected in the very titles of their books: terms like "prison community" and "society of captives" indicate predominant stress on the prison as a self-contained unit.

Since the publication of Sykes' book, a continuous stream of works has appeared on the prison as a social system; unlike the years following Clemmer's contribution, no dearth in publication can be discerned. For a while those who followed Sykes were large concerned with Sykes' question, that of the conditions giving rise to an inmate subculture.[2] But in the last few years a shift of emphasis seems to have taken place.

Rather than being preoccupied with explaining the presence of various aspects of an inmate subculture, prison sociologists have recently stressed that the inmate subculture by no means exists in the same form and with the same strength in all kinds of institutions, and that various conditions place limits on the subcultural response to the pains of imprisonment. This third phase, in which refinement of earlier theory has been the order of the day, is partly found in further case studies of single institutions (Giallombardo 1966), but also in broader, comparative research projects (Street 1965, Street et al. 1966, Cline 1968). In both types of research, there now seems to be a slight concern with the ways in which external institutional relations may influence internal arrangements. Giallombardo discusses the possibility that general sex roles in the outside world may, upon being "brought" into the prison, influence the particular response which inmates show on the inside. Her excellent discussion is based on a study of a women's prison. where inmates showed a response to the pains of imprisonment quite different from that observed in institutions for men. In their broad comparative analysis of seven institutions for juvenile delinquents, Street et al. devote a chapter to the "external strategies" of chief executives in correctional establishments, pointing out that "external demands and transactions create the general conditions to which the internal program must be adjusted." However, these discussions are still exceptions to the rule. The majority of researchers continue to view the penal institution as a more or less self-contained unit. The present essay is an attempt to break with this tradition.

So far the problem of the essay has been stated in very general terms. More precise y, I shall focus on *the ways in which direct top-level exte nal communication, between penal institutions and other organizations, may influence the further internal communication of information gained outside.* In other words, I shall discuss the direct communication with other organizations that takes place along senior-staff institutional boundaries, and the ways in which that boundary process may influence inside penetration of information communicated from the outside. In still other words: internal sharing of information from the outside has traditionally been viewed as a purely internal process. By contrast, I shall relate the internal process to the top-level communication with outside organizations, through which the information was obtained in the first place. I shall indicate the ways in which the latter process may influence the former.

The concepts of "communication," "top-level personnel," and "outside organization" need further comment. By *communication* I mean the sharing of information. The definition, which actually was implied in the above paragraph, hides a number of complexities. Briefly, "sharing" refers to any transfer of information to another individual, whether through face-to-face contact or more distant means, and whether or not the other individual represents a larger social group. By "information" I mean any content of meaning: requests for support and help, indications of likes and dislikes, or what have you. In sum, communication is a social relationship in which meaning is conveyed. There are several reasons for my concentrating on the dimension of communication. For one thing, I have for a long time been personally fascinated by communication processes, especially face-to-face interpersonal communication in intimate situations. As I shall try to show later on, much of the communication involving people in penal institutions is of a face-to-face kind in contexts of intimacy. Over and above my personal interest, earlier penal research has indicated that communication is extremely important when it comes to understanding other aspects of organizational life (see for example McCleery 1960). Furthermore, prison administrators as well as people in lower ranks of penal institutions often refer to communication as being a thorny organizational problem. But while earlier researchers have referred to internal communication as important, I shall add the dimension of external communication. And while prison employees are often not reflectively conscious of any relationship between external and internal communication, I shall address the problem of whether the two may be viewed as parts of a single system.

By *top-level* personnel I mean the chief executive and his closest collaborators. In the penal institutions studied here, "closest collaborators" are defined as those who are members of the chief executive's "council." The exact positions involved will be described later. There are several reasons for concentrating on the communications of this particular group, the most important being that the external communications of senior staff members are probably particularly consequential for institutional structure and change in general. Note that I shall deal with internal sharing of external information primarily as it occurs *among* the senior staff members themselves. Internal sharing with lower-level staff and with inmates will not be discussed in detail, though something will be said about it.

What is meant by an *outside, or external, organization*? By "organization" I mean a social system which has a formal hierarchy of authority, and which is devoted primarily to the attainment of specific goals. (By including "formal hierarchy" in the definition of "organization," goal-oriented social systems which are only informal—such as criminal gangs—are excluded.) The question of "externality" of one organization in relation to another raises the whole complex issue of organizational boundaries. In this essay, organizational boundaries are defined in terms of formal separation. "Formal" separation (which strictly speaking is a matter of degree) stands for separation in terms of official hierarchies of authority. If social relationships A, B, and C are largely or fully separate, in terms of an official hierarchy of authority, from relationships X, Y, and Z, and if the two sets of relationships satisfy the other criteria of "organizations," we shall talk of "separate" organizations. Usually the separateness of an organization is symbolized by a distinct official designation or name. In borderline cases, which can certainly be found, it may be useful to talk of "subsystems" within inclusive organizations. By defining organizational boundaries, and thereby externality, in these terms, I leave open questions such as degree of overlap in concrete membership, degree of physical proximity, degree to which systems are subjectively separated by the participants, degree of organizational freedom and subordination (a ship is in many ways subordinate to the shipping firm, but the two are still almost fully separate in terms of official hierarchies), and—crucial in the present context—degree of communication. These questions are viewed as empirical rather than definitional.

Two further features of the research problem should be emphasized. First, I am going to concentrate on the ways in which direct, top-level external communication *may* influence internal sharing of information gained outside. The implication is that a set of hypotheses—or one general hypothesis, depending on the point of view—rather than definitive results will be presented. Answering a research question with a hypothesis is perhaps slightly unorthodox. According to the standard recipe, hypotheses should be *tested* in research, and sociological analysis should lead to verification or falsification. However, the standard recipe presupposes that a well developed theoretical framework exists prior to the study. As indicated already, the general area of organizational relations with the social environment is underdeveloped. My hypothesis therefore developed gradually, as the study proceeded, and as so often in social science, it received its final form during the analysis of data after the completion of research.

Secondly, though I am going to stress how external communication may influence internal communication, this of course does not preclude the possibility that internal communication patterns may influence external relations. This possibility will also be discussed, and I shall try to show that external and internal communication may constitute a system of mutually reinforcing tendencies.

Organizational elites are generally few in number. Sociological studies of such groups must therefore rely on depth and quality of information rather than on quantity of people interviewed or observed. The data to be considered in this essay stem from the following sources:

1. Detailed interviews with all of the senior staff members, as well as a few other key officers, in two major penal institutions for male offenders in one of the Scandinavian countries: a maximum-security prison and a medium-security establishment. A description of the institutions will be given below. Twenty-three staff members were interviewed in the two institutions. Quite a few were interviewed twice; some were consulted a number of times on specific issues and questions.

The main interview with each staff member varied somewhat in length, the average lasting 2.1 hours. No interview lasted less than an hour and a half. In all but four interviews, detailed notes were taken during the interview session. In the four cases where notes were not taken (the interview situation made note-taking inadvisable), detailed summaries were dictated on tape from memory as soon after the interview as possible. Summaries and interpretations were also dictated after many of the other interviews. It should be mentioned that I knew almost all of the senior staff members in one institution and several of those in the other very well beforehand. In connection with an earlier study, I had spent about a year and a half as a participant observer in the medium-security institution (one year of intensive observation; six months of visiting at regular intervals), and had had considerable contact with selected staff members in the maximum security prison. This made the interview situation comfortable and relaxed, especially in the medium-security institution, and I feel fairly certain that in all but a very few cases the interviewees were very open and honest with me.

2. Participation in senior staff meetings in the two institutions (primarily in the medium-security institution), and fairly continuous association with senior staff members, for a period of two months. I had lunch with staff members, had coffee with them, discussed specific inmates with them, and participated in their general gossip. Observations and impressions were dictated every evening.

3. Interviews with representatives of some of the organizations which constitute the organizational environment of the two penal institutions. The interviews varied in content; to a considerable extent they were adapted to the situation of specific informants. Sixteen individuals were interviewed in nine organizations or sections of organizations. Notes were taken during all but three interviews. The average interview lasted 1.5 hours; only two interviews lasted less than an hour. The organizations were selected in a somewhat *ad hoc* fashion, in the light of advice from penal staff members concerning organizations they found functionally important. The interviews were intended to clarify the data gathered in the penal institutions. An exact listing of the organizations is given in Appendix I, which provides detailed information on the general correctional system in the Scandinavian country concerned. Suffice it here to say that ten of the interviews were conducted in one particularly important organization responsible for supervision of inmates on parole. The exploratory nature of the present research made the *ad hoc* procedure advisable: more conclusive studies may later be geared

toward a systematic survey of the correctional network in general.

4. As mentioned already, I had spent about a year and a half as a participant observer in the medium-security institution included in the present study. During the earlier study, I attended a large number of staff meetings and had a large number of lengthy conversations and interviews with senior staff members (in addition to becoming intimately acquainted with inmates and lower-level staff members). The earlier study provided me with a rich background for the study of external and internal communication, and with an absolutely essential context for the interpretation of interview data. I shall return to this point in greater detail in Chapter II.

During and after the earlier study, I also got to know personally quite a few individuals in the environment of the two penal institutions: parole agents, a few judges, members of the prosecuting authority, and employees in the Prison Bureau. (The Prison Bureau is a department within the Ministry of Justice, and the highest decision-making body in the prison system. Details may be found in Appendix I.) For the purposes of the present study, my knowledge of some of the employees in the Prison Bureau proved to be particularly important. As we shall see later, institutional relations with this particular organization are especially touchy, and though institution staff members were very open about it, I soon found that formal interviews with responsible (and frequently criticized) members of the Prison Bureau gave little in terms of convincing data. I decided not to press matters, and rather to rely on my general and informal knowledge of a few of the Bureau members. Since this knowledge was not obtained as part of an explicit research project, I find it unethical to report it in detail. But I see nothing wrong in using the knowledge to counter-check information gained through regular research channels, and to sort out reliable from unreliable information.

Before concluding the present chapter, descriptive background information will be given on the two penal institutions in which the research problem was explored. The two institutions, which are located near the country's capital city, will be given the fictitious names of *Maximum Security* and *Medium Security*. They were selected partly because they are representative of two prevalent types of contemporary penal institutions: the traditional prison and the treatment-oriented facility. *Maximum Security* is a standard maximum-security prison, while *Medium Security* is a mildly treatment-oriented establishment. Though generalization beyond the two specific institutions cannot strictly speaking be made, it is at least satisfying to know that we are dealing with core types of organizations.

Maximum Security has been in use for over one hundred years. It was built according to the Philadelphia prison system. The prison has a "star form," with four major wings meeting in a center. The institution is surrounded by a high brick wall, and to the present writer it has a very sinister, though interesting, outside appearance. Having the traditional grimness of an old-fashioned close-custody prison, it does not appear any more inviting on the inside. Though the prison has been modernized in several respects (most importantly, a wing containing workshops has been added to the building), the basic principles of the Philadelphia system are still quite apparent. Above all, and despite staff attempts to counteract it, inmates' life in the institution is characterized by considerable isolation. The number of inmates is about two hundred thirty, and at any one time some sixty inmates work in their cells, owing to shortage of adequate shops. Several evenings a week there are educational programs and leisure-time activities which all inmates may attend. However, owing to lack of space, only relatively small proportions of the inmates are outside their cells on other evenings. As in most other penal institutions in the country concerned, all inmates have individual cells. The standard cells have a small barred window high up on the wall. Toilet facilities are virtually non-existent, the cells being furnished with buckets for the purpose. Though facilities for exercise of course exist, the yard appears lean and quarters cramped.

The institution is headed by a governor with a degree in law. In the Scandinavian country concerned, a governor of a penal institution has rather considerable official authority. Though delegation of authority is possible, he can make decisions concerning all institutional questions covered by the Prison Regulations, unless the Regulations specifically state that the decision must be made by someone else (such as by the Prison Bureau). The governor of *Maximum Security* has tried to open new informal lines of communication between the governor's office and the rest of the prison. He is often to be seen in the cell block and in the shops, and he has instituted the practice of having recurrent small-group discussion meetings for lower-level staff, headed by senior staff members. Prior to his employment in *Maximum Security*, the governor had served as a staff member in the Prison Bureau and as the assistant governor of a regional prison.

At the time of the study, the rest of the senior staff in *Maximum Security* consisted of an assistant governor, a psychiatrist, a minister, three social workers, a welfare officer, a head teacher (supervisor of the educational program), and an inspector of the guards (the highest-ranking custodial officer). The assistant governor held degrees in law and nursing. At the time of the study, he had been in the institution for only a few months. The psychiatrist had had wide experience from a variety of mental hospitals and clinics, and had also served as a psychiatrist in *Medium Security*. All of the senior staff members were interviewed for the present study. In addition, interviews were held with the work supervisor and the governor's secretary.

The distinguishing criterion of a "senior staff member" is

that he or she is an official member of, and has a vote in, the governor's "council." The main purpose of the council is to give advice to the governor, though the governor is also a voting member of the council, thus in fact giving advice to himself. Senior staff members normally meet once a week in formal council meetings. The most important questions which are discussed are those of granting release on parole and furloughs. Under certain conditions, specified in Appendix I, the final decision concerning release and furlough is made by the governor upon advice from the council; under others, the decision is made by the Prison Bureau on the basis of a recommendation from the governor. The governor can make decisions or send recommendations which are at variance with the opinion of the rest of the council, but in a majority of cases he agrees with the others. In *Maximum Security*, discussion at the council meeting is fairly free and informal, and contrasting opinions are apparently expressed rather often. In addition to the council meetings, more informal senior staff meetings are held twice a week. At these meetings, internal matters are discussed (most important are the day-to-day reports from the various cell blocks). Furthermore, senior staff members often see each other on a casual basis during working hours. The social workers, the head teacher, and the welfare officer (or psychologist) have offices located next to each other on the top floor, and they generally have lunch together. At times the minister, whose office is located on the first floor, likes to join them. There is no canteen in the institution, and the staff members in question have lunch in one of the offices. The governor and the psychiatrist have offices located close to each other on the second floor, while the assistant governor and the inspector are located on the first floor. The governor and the assistant governor at times have lunch together, but generally the staff members on the top floor seemed to constitute more of a solidary group than those on other floors.

Medium Security, the other penal institution included in the study, was originally designed as a low-security prison for women. Recently a maximum-security section surrounded by a high wall was added to the institution. At the same time the low-security section—from then on known as "The Old House"—was modernized.

To an outsider, the institution gives far less of a stern appearance than does *Maximum Security*. Workshops and assembly rooms for inmates are adequate. Therefore, the daily isolation is less pronounced than in *Maximum Security*. Furthermore, the physical structure of *Medium Security* appears much more inviting. The cells have large (though barred) windows and modern furniture, the courtyard in the low-security section is fairly spacious, and next to the maximum-security section there is a small farm and some hothouses where trusties can work.

At the time of the study, the institution had a total of about ninety inmates. New inmates are generally held in the maximum-security section for a period of time, whereupon they may be transferred to "The Old House." The latter section is more popular among the inmates. The two sections are connected by a long tunnel, and each section has separate workshops and other facilities. All senior staff officers are located on the two top floors of the low-security building.

The governor of the institution is a teacher and a psychologist by training. His official authority is pretty much like that of the governor of *Maximum Security*. In many ways, however, his actual situation is different. He came to his institution in a time of crisis. Six years prior to the present study, the previous governor died of a heart attack in his office. He left behind an institution impaired by a deep internal conflict between the treatment staff and the administrative-custodial staff. For six dramatic months the institution was headed by a lawyer normally employed as a lower-level executive staff member in the Prison Bureau. He only succeeded in aggravating the conflict. A major reason for his lack of success in reducing the tensions was that the conflict in part consisted in treatment staff opposition to the outside Prison Bureau, represented in the institution through the office of the governor. The present governor, who then arrived, had had prior experience as a teacher and as a governor of the country's only penal institution for youthful offenders. For a time he managed to make the conflict less violent, partly because the treatment staff members looked upon him as something of a savior, and as a psychologist with whom they wanted to "start afresh." However, the tension soon reappeared, and at the time of the present study it was back in full strength. The central issues turned out to be the status of "individual treatment" in the institution and the status of the Prison Bureau as a final decision-making body. The psychiatric team stressed the importance of treating the inmates according to their individual psychological needs, while the governor claimed that inmates had to be handled according to relatively general rules. The psychiatrists emphasized that the authority of the Prison Bureau was too great, especially with regard to questions of release and furloughs, while the governor defended the authority of the Bureau. The important point to be stressed here is that the conflict seemed to develop progressively, and that the free flow of communication between the governor and the psychiatric team was impaired in a similar progressive way.

Medium Security has a relatively high treatment staff/inmate ratio, warranting the term "treatment-oriented institution." At the time of the present study, the treatment staff consisted of two psychiatrists, a psychologist, a minister, and two social workers. The chief psychiatrist (referred to above), a man willing to fight hard for his treatment philosophy, had been in the institution since it opened fifteen years prior to the study. The other psychiatrist had been employed for only two years, but had wide prior experience from mental hospitals and hospital clinics. The psychologist was very new, but the minister had been in the institution for about three years. The latter expressed his views in a very straightforward manner, one of his main points being that furloughs and other rewards should be distributed individually, and not according to any general set of rules. He also strongly felt that *Medium Security* should have a more liberal system of furloughs than a regular prison. In these matters, the psychiatrists and the social workers agreed completely with him. The governor, on the other hand, disagreed quite strongly. The inspector of the guards, who had had long experience as a social worker in the institution, appeared to agree with the treatment staff, but not without reservations and qualifications.

As in *Maximum Security*, all of the council staff members (listed above) were interviewed for the present study. In addition, interviews were held with the work supervisor, the governor's secretary, and the captain of the guards (the second-highest-ranking custodial officer).

As in *Maximum Security,* council meetings are held once a week, the most important topics for discussion being questions of release and of furloughs. Discussion is even more informal than in *Maximum Security.* As in *Maximum Security,* regular staff meetings are held twice a week. In addition to the council members, the work supervisor and the captain of the guards are usually present at the latter meetings.

In addition to seeing each other at the above-mentioned staff meetings, senior staff members also associate on a more casual basis. The institution has a canteen for the staff as a whole, where coffee and sandwiches may be purchased. There is, however, a tendency for senior staff members to want to have lunch in small groups in their offices. This is particularly pronounced among the social workers. Their tendency toward separatism is symptomatic of deep-seated and general communication problems in penal establishments, which will be discussed in detail in subsequent chapters.

The remainder of this essay will be divided into four chapters.

Chapter II is essentially introductory. There, a methodological issue relevant to the study will be discussed. Chapters III through V are the core chapters of the essay.

In Chapter III most of the data on the communications of various senior staff members will be presented. The chapter will be organized in a particular fashion. In many exploratory studies, in which hypotheses are developed during and after the research, the reader is presented with bold statements of hypotheses at the outset. As a next step, the hypotheses are then "supported," or given credibility, by selected illustrations. In this essay I shall try to break with this pattern. In Chapter III I shall try, as far as possible, to present data without imposing on them my own theoretical views of external and internal communication. The clause "as far as possible" is important. Any description, however detailed, is necessarily guided by concepts and is thereby selective. The imposition of a theoretical framework is therefore unavoidable; data can never be presented in their "raw" form. Terms such as "descriptive material" and "observational data" should always be read in quotation marks. But an attempt will be made at least to keep the selectivity and imposition of framework at a minimum. Thereby the reader should be better able to judge the merits of generalizations and interpretations offered later on.

If Chapter III intends to keep abstraction at a minimum, the opposite is the case with Chapter IV. In the latter chapter, a few generalizations will first be abstracted from the material presented earlier. Next, these generalizations will be related to each other, forming my interpretive hypothesis concerning the relationship between external and internal communication. But it should be noted that Chapter IV will also include the presentation of some additional data, more easily discussed there than in Chapter III. In short, though I shall try hard to separate "data" from "theory" in this essay, the attempt will not—cannot—be fully successful: the "data" will to some degree imply "theory," and the "theory" will to some degree involve the presentation of "data."

In Chapter V, some concluding theoretical questions will be discussed. The chapter will largely be devoted to the question of generalizing the main interpretive hypothesis to other types of organizations and social settings.

To secure the anonymity of individuals, reviewers and others using material from the present work are asked to be cautious when referring to case material and interview excerpts in Chapters III–V. Note that in order to ensure anonymity, certain insignificant details are changed.

II

A NOTE

ON EMPATHY

AND ERROR

Understanding of motivation . . . consists in placing the act in an intelligible and more inclusive context of meaning. . . . Thus for a science which is concerned with the subjective meaning of action, explanation requires a grasp of the context of meaning.

Max Weber

Sociological studies of complex organizations are frequently criticized by those who work and live in the organizations. Though the specific content of the criticism varies considerably, a few general themes run through much of it. One is that the sociologist is out of touch with real life. His report, it is claimed, does not reflect social reality as it is experienced by those working in the organization. The sociological analysis, the critics argue, is "lifeless."

The sociologist under criticism might disregard this view as merely reflecting the oversensitive defensiveness of the organization member. He may even view the criticism as unintended praise: if his report appears "lifeless" to the organization member, this may be taken to mean that it is "scientific" rather than "just descriptive"; that it is objective, abstract, and focuses on latent phenomena.

Organization members certainly may be defensive, and the aim of the sociological report is rarely that of pure description. Yet I doubt the wisdom of totally disregarding the criticism of the organization member. In part, the member's criticism points to a serious difficulty in current sociological research. "Look," the organization member says, "you're writing as if you were sitting on the moon rather than down here with us. I don't recognize my prison (plant, hospital) at all in what you're saying, it's just hanging in the air. I don't recognize myself, my colleagues, or our inmates (workers, patients); we're described as if we had no meat on our bones." When making such a statement, the organization member in effect brings a crucial methodological message to the attention of the researcher.

On the basis of observations made in the field, the sociologist attempts to offer a few abstractions concerning the phenomenon he has studied. As a second step, he attempts to relate various abstractions to each other (for example by correlating variables), and to set forth explanations and/or predictions on the basis of these relationships. But the crucial step of relating abstractions ("variables," "factors," "tendencies," "characteristics," etc.) to each other is not automatic: it involves a good deal of *interpretation* on the part of the sociologist. "Interpretation" is here taken in a wide sense, as covering the general process of viewing the abstractions in question in relation to the wider body of sociological knowledge and belief. Interpretation may range from the implicit and informal to the highly formal and explicit; in any case it is there. *The trouble, however, is that sociologists often try to interpret their abstractions without reference to the context of meaning.* "Context of meaning" refers to the subjective frame of reference—unconscious or conscious, implicit or explicit, idiosyncratic or shared—of the participants in question.

Insofar as the context of meaning is not taken into account when interpretations are made, sociological statements about causes and consequences have low explanatory power and low predictive value. Essentially, this is the significant message that the organization member's criticism contains.

There are exceptions to the neglect of the context of meaning. The two sociological traditions, stemming from Max Weber and Edmund Husserl respectively, stress the concept of "meaning." Alfred Schutz, whom we briefly consider below, may be said to combine the two traditions. Nevertheless, the neglect of meaning-contexts by sociologists is sufficiently pronounced and general to warrant serious attention. The present chapter is intended only as a reminder of its importance.

Let me give some examples from organizational research to illustrate the importance of the context of meaning, and the dangers of disregarding it.

Some years ago I took part in constructing a questionnaire designed for inmates of penal institutions. The questionnaire, intended to measure such things as inmates' interaction patterns and their responses to the pains of incarceration, was administered to convicts in a wide range of Scandinavian penal establishments. Playing around with some of the results, I was tempted to view tabulations of answers as automatically showing "differences" and "similarities" between various institutions. Yet the answers were the inmates' own abstract summaries of views and feelings about institutional life; hence the tabulated frequencies could be given no reasonable interpretation without detailed reference to the context of meaning—to the views and expectations of inmates in specific institutions, and to the broader cultural, and thereby defining, setting.

In more detail: One of the questions in the questionnaire read: "How often do you have a fairly long talk with guards in this institution?" The question was designed to measure an aspect of staff-inmate interaction. By the researchers, outsiders to the institutions included in the study, the question was assumed to have roughly the same meaning to inmates regardless of institutional context. This assumption is hardly warranted. The issue of whether a given contact between guard and inmate is termed "a fairly long talk" depends considerably on the perceived chances of having contact. The perceived chances probably vary between maximum-security prisons, open institutions, and so on. Probable variations in perceived chances of contact must be considered when results from a question of this kind are interpreted.

Another set of questions in the questionnaire was intended to tap "anti-staff attitudes" in various institutions and countries. The questions were constructed as "hypothetical conflict situations": simple stories involving conflicts between inmates and staff were presented, and the inmates were asked (among other things) to express their personal opinion about the conflicts. Again it is tempting to view tabulations of answers as automatically showing "differences" and "similarities" between institutions and countries. Again, however, it is essential first to interpret the answers in the light of the context of meaning. What to the outsider is the "same" hypothetical staff-inmate conflict, may very well have differing significance to inmates in different institutions and countries. If so, similarities between frequency distributions may conceal differences in what the inmates intend their responses to say. Similarly, differences between frequency distributions may conceal similarities in intention.

A well-known theoretical contribution to complex organizations may provide a second example. Etzioni's comparative organizational analysis is geared toward producing hypotheses concerning differences and similarities between broad classes of complex organizations (Etzioni 1961). By way of introduction, Etzioni presents a classification of complex organizations. The classification is arrived at through a cross-tabulation of (1) types of power employed by higher-level participants and (2) types of organizational involvement on the part of lower-level participants. Three types of power—coercive, remunerative and normative—and three types of involvement—alienative, calculative and moral—yield nine possible types of so-called "compliance patterns." Three diagonal types—coercive/alienative, remunerative/calculative, and normative/moral—are so-called "congruent types." They are believed to be more frequent than others, so that most complex organizations may be classified within one of them. They are referred to as *predominantly coercive, predominantly utilitarian,* and *predominantly normative* organizations respectively. Next, Etzioni sets forth a series of hypotheses concerning differences between the three major classes of organizations. He discusses differences in variables such as consensus, communication, socialization, recruitment, cohesion, etc. In some measure, he also sets forth hypotheses concerning differences within each class of organizations. The analysis is systematic, and solidly grounded in empirical research whenever possible. Yet, some of the comparisons do not appear immediately and fully convincing. I think the reason is that the author at times relates and manipulates variables without considering the context of meaning within various organizations. Let me illustrate in more detail.

Etzioni defines "alienation" as an "intense negative orientation" toward the organization (p. 10), and "coercive power" as (the threat of) application "of physical sanctions such as infliction of pain, deformity, or death; generation of frustration through restriction of movement; . . . and the like" (p. 5). When considering predominantly coercive organizations only, he makes the reasonable argument that under otherwise equal conditions, we should expect alienation among lower-level members to increase as coercion is increasingly applied by higher-level members. On the basis of this hypothesis, he goes on to predict that the alienation produced in "typical correctional institutions" will be less than that produced in "typical prisons." My own experience from one penal institution of the former kind makes me question the latter prediction. From the point of view of the uninitiated outsider, coercion may well be less pronounced in the typical correctional institution than in the typical prison. But *degree of coercion may appear quite different when the context of meaning is considered:* inmates in correctional institutions may subjectively find themselves more coerced than those in regular prisons. For example, the former may find their freedom particularly restricted in view of the enticements of freedom following from medium security conditions. They may also find their freedom especially restricted due to personalized "provocations" from the treatment staff. As a consequence they may, at least during certain phases of their institutional career, be more alienated from the organization than their fellow inmates in regular prisons. It should be noted that recent comparative research in fact indicates an institutional difference in perception of power in the direction I have suggested. Interestingly, the research in question seems to suggest a somewhat greater degree of alienation on the part of inmates in correctional settings than of those in regular prisons (Cline 1968, pp. 177–78).[3]

What is the relevance of this discussion for the present study?

Consider first that in a study based on interviews alone, it is extremely difficult to gain an adequate understanding of the context of meaning, and correspondingly easy to overlook the context as irrelevant. In more detail: Interviews are necessarily of limited length; furthermore, interviews constitute only one source of information, and the researcher relying on interviews alone therefore covers only a limited span of information. Together, these two aspects of the interview technique (which are even more apparent when question-naires are used) make for poor understanding of the context of meaning. Obtaining an understanding of the context of meaning generally (1) takes time—usually much more study than that allowed within the framework of an interview study, and (2) requires a broad span of information—usually much broader than that given by interviews alone. And when lacking a close grasp of the context of meaning, it is tempting to overlook it as unimportant, and to proceed by manipulating abstractions as if they had some kind of intrinsic significance.

The present study to a considerable extent relies on interviews, conducted over a two-month period in a few selected organizations. The study is therefore potentially vulnerable to criticism for inadequate understanding of and reference to the context of meaning. But as mentioned in Chapter I, I fortunately also had access to information obtained from other sources. A number of observations were made during the two months—I spent a good deal of non-interview time in the two institutions. But more important for the present purposes are one-and-a-half years of intensive prior participation in one of the two penal institutions in question, briefer but intensive association with staff members in the other institution, and non-research-oriented knowledge of relevant individuals in the institutional environment. Without this additional information, I would never have dared to rely on the interview technique as a way of gathering information about communication. The additional information not only provides another set of data to be reported, or a "general background" for the construction of intelligent questions to the informants. In addition, and much more importantly, it provides a base for understanding the context of meaning within which abstractions from interview data must be interpreted.

Precisely where and how will the context of meaning be

taken into account? First a few words about the *where* of the question. The context of meaning will be taken into account throughout the essay, but particularly in Chapter IV. This is the point at which abstractions will be set forth and related most explicitly. There I shall point (1) to the major mode of senior staff communication with outside organizations, (2) to certain striking deficiencies in inside sharing of information gained outside, and (3) to possible causal relationships between mode of external communication and inadequacies in internal communication. In relating mode of external communication and inadequacies in internal communication, consideration of the context of meaning will be crucial. The causal link which is hypothesized becomes reasonable when we consider the actor's frame of reference, thus capturing the way in which outside organizations and inside colleagues appear to the man or woman who in fact performs the communication.

How will the context of meaning be taken into account? Extensive prior knowledge is, as I have pointed out, absolutely essential in providing a basis for understanding the context of meaning. However, prior knowledge can rarely if ever be pointed to as direct "evidence," for it is usually obtained for other than a research purpose and under other conditions. Furthermore, it is doubtful indeed whether it makes sense to say that we observe a point of view, a perspective, a subjective meaning, "directly." We observe behavior, including oral statements such as answers to attitude questionnaires, etc., not the "meaning" attached to the behavior. But if prior knowledge cannot be pointed to as direct evidence, it can at least be used indirectly: as a general basis for empathizing with the participants in question, as a basis for making fairly accurate guesses concerning the point of view and experience of the actor, as a basis for *imagining* what a given actor would think and feel under given conditions. *This is the primary way in which the context of meaning will be taken into account in Chapter IV. In causally relating external and internal communication, I shall imagine that I am a staff member, and try to depict how communications would then appear to me.* In short, consideration of the context of meaning will imply a good deal of inference. If further research involving harder data shows the correlation and the time-sequence of variations in variables predicted by the hypothesis, it should mean that my inferences have in fact been intelligent.

Before closing this chapter, the reader should probably be warned: as a method of grasping the subjective meaning-context of the actor, the process of empathizing with him—of imagining that one is he—has been severely criticized through the modern history of social thought. Various influential schools of sociology, from extreme positivism with its emphasis on reliability to radical phenomenology with its Husserlian bracketing of the natural world, have rejected the method as "unscientific."

Yet as far as I can see, no school of sociology has provided any better method. The hard-headed positivist has been more or less uninterested in the whole problem, which has led him to a context-free sociology of the kind criticized earlier in this chapter. The Weberian social action theorist has definitely been interested, but he has not provided a method that is more valid. Neither has the true phenomenologist.

A detailed exposition of this point would require a careful presentation and critique of the works of Dilthey, Rickert, Windelband, Weber, and others on the one hand, and of Husserl, Scheler, Schutz, Garfinkel, Goffman, et al., on the other. Such a presentation lies far outside the scope of the present essay. However, a few words will be said about Schutz' contribution, because he tried particularly hard to specify a more valid way for social science to study the subject's standpoint (Schutz 1932, English edition 1967).

Schutz starts off from the phenomenology of Edmund Husserl and the sociology of Max Weber. Husserl's phenomenology leads him to a radical criticism of Weber's theoretical concepts, especially of Weber's concept of meaning. A point of departure for Schutz is Weber's distinction between observational understanding (*aktuelles Verstehen*) and explanatory understanding (*erklärendes Verstehen*) of subjective meaning. When referring to "observational understanding," Weber apparently had in mind the understanding of the actor's subjective meaning through direct observation of the (behavioral) manifestations of his act. By "explanatory understanding" he apparently meant that subjective meaning may also be grasped in terms of the motive the actor attaches to his act. Schutz spends a number of pages in a critical examination of these and related conceptualizations. First, he rejects "observational understanding" as an inadequate description of what goes on when we try to grasp the subjective meaning of the other:

> Observational understanding of the other person's outward behavior is clearly not enough. . . . These are questions of subjective meaning and cannot be answered by merely watching someone's behavior, as Weber seems to think. On the contrary, we first observe the bodily behavior and then place it within a larger context of meaning. . . . But this context of meaning . . . cannot . . . be identical with the context of meaning in the mind of the actor himself. Let us call it the *objective* context of meaning as opposed to the actor's *subjective* context of meaning. (p. 27).

In other words, when merely observing external behavior, the observer invokes his own meaning-context in interpretation, and not the meaning-context of the actor-subject.

Schutz seems to find the notion of "explanatory understanding" more acceptable, but far too unrefined to be a fully adequate recipe for insight into the subject's context of meaning. He introduces a number of nuances and distinctions which he considers essential. In general, he seems to feel that the discovery of a man's motive is no clear-cut guide to his subjective meaning. Schutz concludes that "both types of understanding start out from an objective meaning-context. The understanding of subjective meaning has no place in either" (p. 29).

The present discussion of Schutz' critique of Weber is by no means exhaustive; it is only intended as a brief background for his own suggestion. What, then, does Schutz himself suggest as a way of studying the subjective meaning of the actor? For anyone hoping for a method going beyond the simple mental placement of oneself in the actor's position, the result is disappointing. After his lengthy and involved critique of Weber, Schutz simply concludes that "we put ourselves in the place of the actor and identify our lived experiences with his" (p. 114). To be sure, he hastily adds that "it might seem that we are here repeating the error of the well-known 'projective' theory of empathy. . . . But, if we look more closely, we will see that our theory has nothing in common with the empathy theory. . . . We start out from the general thesis of the other person's flow of duration, while the projective theory of empathy jumps from the mere fact of empathy to the belief in other minds by an act of blind faith" (p. 114). When read in context, however, Schutz does not explicate how putting oneself "in the place of the actor" and considering the actor's "flow of duration" (a concept taken from Bergson) differ *in principle* from the "projective theory of empathy." I, at least, fail to find any other method in Schutz' main work than a refined and critical use of the projective one. In the final chapter of his study, he does discuss the ideal-type method, suggesting—in line with Max Weber—this method as a way of bridging between objective and subjective meaning (pp. 241–42). Yet projective empathy—the mental placement of oneself in the position of the actor—seems to be presupposed despite his vigorous denial of it.

Schutz may be right in assuming that the Observer's imagination of the Subject's experience necessarily varies from the Subject's own experience—if nothing else in that it is imagination and empathy rather than personalized meaning. Thus, subjective experience may be truly accessible only to the actor himself (pp. 114–15), and projective empathy may at best be a highly imperfect method. But however imperfect, it is all we have. Rather than disregarding the subjective context of meaning because the method is imperfect, I therefore prefer to rely on the method to throw at least some light on the subject's experience.

To repeat, the basis of my empathy with senior staff members in penal institutions consists of long-term participant observation in one of the institutions, and of general "wandering" for several years within the more inclusive correctional setting. The importance of this general background may now be stated in Schutz-like (if not Schutz' own) terms: it provides a basis of interpreting interview material gathered at a single point in time in terms of the time dimension and in terms of a broad range of actions on the part of the individuals involved. In turn, this implies two important requirements for a *critical* use of empathy in social research: those of having *long-term knowledge* of whole *configurations of acts* on the part of the actors in question. When relying on long-term knowledge of whole configurations of acts one avoids what Schutz feared: jumping to the belief in other minds "by an act of blind faith."

COMMUNICATIONS

OF SENIOR

STAFF MEMBERS

At three o'clock Saturday afternoon the lawyer called, telling the social worker about the accident. The road had been wet and slippery, and on her way home from visiting her husband in the prison, Ketil's wife had driven off the road. She was alive, the lawyer said, but badly bruised, and had been taken to the hospital. There was no one to take care of the child and the farm, and the lawyer felt there was good reason to give Ketil a furlough to take care of things. The social worker could not promise anything, except to try. The first thing she did was to call the hospital, to find out how badly hurt Ketil's wife actually was. It turned out to be quite serious: she had broken her jaw. Calling the local Social Board, the social worker found that, true enough, there was no one in the home to take care of Ketil's boy, let alone the farm. The social worker then called the police in Ketil's home town, to find out what they thought of a furlough for Ketil. The police did not object; they knew Ketil, and did not consider him dangerous. With this information, the social worker felt that the case for recommending a welfare furlough was strong. By now the hour was late, so the prison governor had to be called at his home. He was not convinced right away that Ketil could safely be given a welfare furlough—after all, Ketil was the kind of person who might get into trouble. But after hearing the details of the case, he consented, and granted Ketil a three-day furlough. With the decision in hand, the social worker again called the lawyer and the police station, telling them about it. Ketil got his welfare furlough at 10:30 that night, just in time to catch the last train.

But Ketil's furlough had an aftermath. When the three days were up, he called the prison and begged for an extension—the farm just could not be left alone. An extension could only be granted by the Prison Bureau. After an improvised and rushed council discussion, the governor called the Director of Prisons, presenting the case as best he could. The directors agreed. After another few days, the governor actually managed to have the extended furlough transformed to a temporary release. This time, the argument about the farm would not be enough: the governor knew he had to stress the wife's illness much more strongly. At 4:30 p.m. on Saturday, a week after Ketil got his first furlough, the social worker received word by telephone that a one-month temporary release had been granted.

The above sequence of incidents occurred during a brief working week of a prison social worker and a prison governor. The sequence constituted only a small part of their work during that week. From one point of view, the sequence is atypical: welfare furloughs and temporary releases are not often granted to inmates. But from another vantage point it is in fact representative of the kind of work these people continually engage in. The welfare furlough transformed into a temporary release could have been a furlough of a more regular kind, or a release on parole, or an extended visit. The concrete circumstances would then have been different, and time perhaps less pressing, but the sense of urgency would still have been there. So would the basic processes of gathering information, forming recommendations, and making decisions. Above all, the many outside organizations involved in the process would still have been brought in through *direct, person-to-person contact*. We shall return to this in detail below.

The question now is how to represent communication processes such as those illustrated above in a systematic form. In this chapter, the senior staff members of the two penal institutions will be grouped into six major categories, and described in view of the following five broad questions.

In what areas, if any, is the staff member a specialist in direct, external communication? More precisely, in relation to which outside organizations, if any, is he among the most important (if not the only) direct staff communicators? By definition, the role of "specialist" cannot be shared equally by all senior staff members in an institution. At the same time, however, the role is somewhat loosely defined to include more than just the full-scale communication monopolizer: the role can be shared by "several"; to qualify, the incumbent must be *among the most important* direct communicators with the organization in question. It is implied that "importance" is measured as a given staff member's frequency of contact with a given organization, relative to other staff members' frequency of contact with that organization. I shall also say something about a given staff member's frequency of contact with a given organization relative to the *same* staff member's contact with *other* organizations, but this should not be confused with our measure of "importance."[4] Note that though a communication specialist almost always communicates on the basis of official institutional legitimation, this does not follow by definition. By definition, a communication specialist may be communicating illegitimately. Note also that staff members who are equally important as communicators with given organizations will be said to "share" the role of specialist even if they differ in terms of content of communication. In other words, the specific communication task does not define a staff member as a specialist.

What is the content of the staff member's direct communication with the outside organization in which he specializes? For example, to what extent are requests and answers being communicated, and what is actually being requested and answered?

What is the form of the staff member's direct communication with the organizations in question? Most important, to what extent is direct communication informal (not specified in written regulations) and personal (oriented to specific individuals in other organizations rather than to the organizations in general)?

What, in summary form, is the staff member's general view of his communication with the organizations in question? More precisely, how satisfactory or unsatisfactory does he find his direct communications with "his" organizations?

What is the staff member's view of his communication with relevant organizations in relation to which other staff members are communication specialists? More precisely, does he view his lack of direct access to these organizations as a problem or not? By "relevant" organizations I mean those which the staff member in question considers influential in relation to his own role performance.

Answers to the first four questions tell us something about the staff member's direct communications with outside organizations. Answers to the fifth question tell us, by implication, something about the further inside sharing of information obtained outside: the more difficult a staff member finds his lack of direct access to outside organizations, the more obstructed indirect communication may be inferred to be. But it should be noted that answers to the fifth question are not our only measure of inside sharing: I shall also report results from direct questions and observations concerning the staff member's tendency to share information with colleagues. However, the latter material is more easily reported in connection with the generalizations and interpretations in Chapter IV.

I shall first describe staff members who are communication specialists in relation to a relatively large number of outside organizations, and follow with an account of those whose boundary-activities are less widespread. It should be noted, however, that with the data in hand a precise ranking at times cannot be made. When ranking in terms of boundary importance is uncertain, roles will be described in the order of their regular rank inside the institution. Furthermore, a few senior staff members who are clearly regarded as "less important" in terms of regular rank will not be introduced till the end of the chapter. Parallel staff members in the two institutions will be compared and contrasted as we proceed. When parallel staff members show similar patterns, no differentiation between them will be made.

THE GOVERNORS

Realms of specialization in external communication

The governor of a penal institution in the Scandinavian country concerned is a specialist in direct communication with several external organizations. His importance relative to colleagues is particularly clear in relation to *other organizations within the prison system* — the Prison Bureau and other penal institutions. As we shall see later, he shares his responsibility in relation to other penal institutions with a few other senior staff members. In relation to the Prison Bureau, however, he has close to a monopoly on direct communication. According to the express wishes of senior Bureau members, communication with the Bureau is to be left to the governor or others in his office. To a considerable extent, this is followed in practice.

Direct communication between a governor's office and the Prison Bureau is frequent, although precise indications are hard to give. One of the governors interviewed for this study claimed that communication with the Bureau varies from once a week to several times per day, by letter, telephone, or in face-to-face contact. The other governor volunteered "at least once a day" as his general estimate. Estimates of this kind, of course, should be interpreted with great caution; casual observations suggest that these are low. A governor's communication with penal institutions is less frequent.

The governors are also responsible to some degree for direct communication with some official organizations outside the prison system, such as the Prosecuting Authority, the police, the Supervisory Board (an independent committee appointed by the Ministry of Justice, which inspects penal institutions and listens to inmate complaints), and the Ombudsman. However, the governor's role as a specialist in relation to these organizations is in part less clear (communication with the police is often delegated to the inspector, the captain or the social workers; communication with the prosecutor is at times channeled through the social workers), and his frequency of communication is in any case very low relative to his contacts within the prison system. Furthermore, a governor is even less of a specialist in relation to other official and semi-official organizations, such as state and municipal welfare agencies, treatment institutions of various kinds, and welfare agencies in charge of supervising parolees. Direct communication with these organizations is to a considerable extent left to the social workers and the psychiatrists, though written communication does often go through the governor's office. Furthermore, direct communication with private organizations is largely performed by other staff members. Religious and other charitable organizations, and profit-organizations that employ inmates or provide the institution with work assignments and supplies, are generally in direct communication with the social workers, the minister, the welfare officer, or the work superintendent, depending on the particular task in question (see Appendix I).

Since the relative importance of the governor as a direct communicator is clearest in relation to other organizations within the prison system, I shall largely concentrate on his boundary activities as a specialist in this setting.

What is the content and form of the governors' communication with organizations within the prison system? Below, content and form will be discussed together.

Content and form of communication

The governors' communication with the Prison Bureau is partly formal and impersonal. That is, communication is stipulated by explicit, written rules, and is addressed to and from "the Ministry" or the "Prison Bureau" as whole entities rather than to and from specific individuals. Formal and impersonal communication is almost always written. Inmates' applications for release on parole are sent on with written (positive or negative) recommendations from the council and the governor. Similar written recommendations are sent on when inmates apply for changes in preventive measures, for extended furloughs, etc. As a general principle, when communication between the governor's office and the Bureau implies a decision on the part of the Bureau, the communication should be in writing. Consequently, a large quantity of documents travels between the institutions and the Bureau. Statistical records of these documents are not available, so precise frequencies cannot be given.

Formalized communications by no means stand alone, however. Alongside the stream of formal and impersonal applications, recommendations, and other documents, there is a stream of informal and very personal communication between the governor and/or his secretary and members of the Prison Bureau. Though in principle such communication may be written, it is almost always oral.

First, the governors have frequent informal face-to-face contact with particular members of the Bureau, usually the Prison Director (the head of the prison system). Apparently, this is especially the case for the governor in *Maximum Security,* perhaps because he previously had been employed in the Bureau. But it is also to a considerable extent the case for the governor in *Medium Security*. The face-to-face contact is described as warm, close and very friendly.

> We drop in. You know, we know each other so well; it becomes so informal. These contacts have an awfully personal character.

The face-to-face contact is apparently a two-way process, in the sense that both parties seek each other.

> [The Prison Director] comes here as a matter of routine, and he walks around in the institution and talks and drinks a cup of tea and talks with me, and then we discuss a variety of things. . . . And then I am often down in the Bureau—oh, about twelve times a year I suppose, and that's not counting all of those times I am down there in connection with the building plans for the new prison, and not the regular governors' meetings in the Bureau. Because at such meetings I cannot bring up my special points: I do that more under four eyes with the Director. (Paraphrased from notes taken after the interview.)

What is the content of the informal face-to-face communication? Four major themes may be mentioned. In the first place, the governor tries to defend the general interests of his institution. Typically, he brings up general principles underlying procedures such as release and furlough decisions, trying for example to simplify the work of his staff by suggesting adjustments in underlying guidelines. Such suggestions seem especially likely when new regulations are to be introduced.

We don't talk about the concrete inmate Joe Doe, because I know that wouldn't work. We talk about somewhat more general things, but always things which have concrete relevance to us in our daily work. For example, there are now plans also to let all inmates apply for release on parole after "half time." The idea is that these applications are to be decided by the Prison Bureau . . . and then more letters and so on must go to the Prison Bureau, and that will require a lot of work on our part, and therefore I discuss it with the Prison Director ahead of time and sort of privately. (Paraphrased from notes taken after the interview. For details on "half time" parole, see Appendix I and note 23.)

In the second place, the governor seeks expert interpretation and clarification of correct institutional behavior.

Since the institutions have a common set of regulations, it's important [for the staff] to behave similarly in the various institutions. . . . How to handle packages for inmates, whether or not to allow typewriters in the cells, whether or not to allow birds, etc. Perhaps it sounds ridiculous with such trifles, but it's important to have regulations for such trivial things, and we want to be fair. (Paraphrased from notes taken after the interview.)

Thirdly, the governor sometimes elaborates on his personal opinion concerning individual inmates. For example:

[Cases going to the Prison Bureau] include the decision of the council here and then I attach my personal comments. And then from time to time I follow up orally, in order to get across what I think is correct, and at times I am also asked to come to face-to-face meetings [to explain in more detail].

This excerpt in part contradicts one of the quotes presented above, where it was said that "we don't talk about the concrete inmate Joe Doe." It should be emphasized that the two statements were made by different governors, perhaps having somewhat different policies concerning "Joe Doe." The contradiction is also made less blatant by the fact that the governor who did say he discussed concrete cases with the Director, apparently did so only rather occasionally.

Finally, in the informal face-to-face contacts discussed

here, the Prison Director apparently tries to interpret actions and decisions made by the Prison Bureau. In part, he probably tries to soften criticism which may be raised against the Bureau as final decision-making body. One of the governors explained as follows:

> I think he [the Prison Director] feels a need to tell us where the problem lies. I think this is useful because part of the criticism you feel like leveling against a superior [i.e., the Prison Bureau] is reduced when you hear how things stand behind the curtains. . . . For example, applications which we feel remain there too long— you wonder why they cannot take your own important case faster—and then you hear about personnel problems . . . or they are working on matters which are of far greater societal significance than your little gripe [there you gain insight by direct communication]. And I wouldn't be surprised if the Director is wise enough to come here precisely for that reason.

In both institutions the inmates put enormous pressure on the staff, not only to obtain favorable decisions concerning questions like release, but also to obtain rapid decisions. Staff members, feeling that the Prison Bureau is ultimately responsible for outcome as well as slowness of a decision, in turn criticize the Prison Bureau. This is the criticism which the Prison Director apparently tries to ward off. That he is at times successful may be inferred from the following statement, which is a continuation of the next to the last quote given above:

> And at times [during face-to-face meetings] I have to admit that even if we, or I, have recommended release, I understand the Ministry, who have the final responsibility.

In short, then, in the informal, face-to-face contacts between governors and their chief, the governors defend their general institutional interests, seek clarification of correct behavior, and at times elaborate on their recommendations, while the chief tries to interpret the Bureau's actions and decisions. All of these problems are inadequately taken care of through formal and impersonal communication.

Informal and personalized communication with the Bureau takes place not only in face-to-face contexts but also over the telephone. Though the telephone is used frequently by both governors (and their secretaries), its importance was stressed more strongly by the governor in *Medium Security*. It will be recalled that his face-to-face communication apparently was less frequent than that of the governor in *Maximum Security*.

One of the governors described the informality of his use of the phone in the following words:

> It's impossible to say even approximately how often I have oral contact with the Prison Bureau [but it is very frequent]. It can be a rather impulsive contact: I can sit here with one case and then another swirls around in my mind, and then I grab the telephone, and then you can often have rather long conversations.

The fact that the governor tries to personalize his informal telephone communications is clearly seen in a statement which followed immediately upon the excerpt given above:

> And here is a problem which I think is interesting: most of the positions in [the Bureau] are [not held by permanent people], and that's something I think is terribly unfortunate. One division in the Bureau has had four Heads of Division in twelve years, and every time a new man comes, it takes time before you manage to establish an equally good contact. . . . This is a very poor arrangement. . . . The fact that you [often] have to turn to a new man is important [and difficult].

In terms of initiation, informal and personal communication by telephone is a two-way process, but one of the governors did feel that communication of this kind was initiated most frequently from the institution. Often, the governor's secretary makes the call for his superior. Precise frequencies cannot be given, but judging from very casual observations in the secretaries' offices, there is probably telephone contact with particular individuals in the Bureau several times per day. (Compare this with the governors' own estimates, above.) The content of the communication varies. Frequently, the governor and his secretary try to speed up decision-making in the Bureau, thus in this context discussing concrete cases. In addition, further information concerning specific cases is communicated upon request from the Bureau.

One other feature of the informal and personalized communication with the Prison Bureau should be emphasized. According to both governors, it is not always easy to talk openly to others about the content of the communication. This does not mean that outright secrets are necessarily being communicated, but it does mean that

> . . . these things are somewhat on the confidential side. . . . There are always some things which are . . . somewhat delicate.

The fact that the governor's defense of institutional interests, his attempts to clarify correct institutional behavior, his elaborations of recommendations, and perhaps even the Prison Director's attempts to interpret his actions and decisions, become "delicate" matters to the parties involved will be interpreted at considerable length in Chapter IV.

Unlike communication with the Prison Bureau, which is at least partly formalized and impersonal, the governors' communications with other penal institutions take place in settings which make for almost nothing but informality and personalization.

> In later years we have had the recurrent practice, that we [the prison governors] go away together for a few days, with meetings all day, and then we discuss common problems. . . . And even if it's not regular, the governors have meetings with people from the Bureau, and that's also useful for our work as a whole. That happens three or four times between fall and spring. . . . The Director is very keen on these meetings.

In addition, many governors in the prison system meet personally in other contexts, for example at penological meetings and criminological seminars, and in purely private contexts. Thus they get to know each other very well, especially if they are located in the same geographical area. The governors interviewed for this study referred to "common problems" as the main content of their communication. "Common problems" seem to include the interpretation of regulations, personnel difficulties, and relations with outside organizations such as the courts, the police, the Prosecuting Authority, and the press.

General view of direct communications

What can be said, in summary form, about the governors' degree of satisfaction with their direct communications within the prison system? The material on content and form suggests the possibility of a fairly high degree of satisfaction. When trying to sum up their views on communications, the governors in fact directly expressed satisfaction.

To be sure, they had a somewhat vague feeling that communication between the Prison Bureau and the penal institutions in general might be improved. At the same time, both governors claimed that, personally, they had established very efficient, direct communication lines with the Prison Bureau. After have described his poor relations with the Prosecuting Authority, one of the governors expressed this view in the following manner:

> Now with regard to the Prison Bureau, that's something entirely different; there conditions are quite different. . . . Oh, the Prison Bureau: I'm almost a part of it—it's almost like being at home. (Paraphrased from notes taken after the interview.)

The governor who ranked highest in terms of face-to-face contact with members of the Bureau was also particularly satisfied with his communications. Thus, satisfaction with communication seems to be related to degree of informality and personalization.

Both governors also viewed their communication with

representatives of other penal institutions (usually other governors) as generally "satisfactory." One of them characterized the contact as "lively."

In view of their roles as communication specialists, it is of course possible that the governors presented their communications within the prison system in a more favorable light than their feelings actually warranted. Admittedly, no test of this possibility exists, but it seems unreasonable as a major explanation of their statements indicating satisfactory communication: both governors seemed open and honest, they appeared to feel quite at ease when talking to the researcher (whom they knew well ahead of time), and they talked freely about their external relations.

View of communications with other organizations

What about the governors' views of their communications with organizations outside the prison system, in relation to which they are less clearly, or not at all, communication specialists?

Many organizations outside the prison system are considered relevant by the two governors, and both clearly found their general lack of direct access to these organizations a problem. Both emphasized not only their personal isolation from outside organizations, but isolation of their respective institutions and the prison system in general. As we shall see later, other staff members did have rather frequent contact with some of the organizations referred to by the governors, and were in part rather satisfied with their communications. The governors' description of institutional isolation therefore suggests a strange "unawareness" of the communications of colleagues.

Let us look at the governors' statements and views in more detail. During interviews and informal conversations, as well as in purely non-research contexts, the governor of *Medium Security* repeatedly stressed that he and his institution, as well as the prison system in general, are greatly isolated from organizations outside the prison system. In fact, he said so during my first conversation with him for the present study, when I briefly presented the project to him and told him that I had received the Prison Bureau's permission to carry it out. Quite spontaneously he claimed that the project sounded very interesting to him, because the prison system as a whole sadly lacked contact with outside agencies. He seemed to feel that the prison system existed in a kind of vacuum, to a large extent unintegrated with the rest of the community. He claimed that one reason might be an unwarranted fear of the prison system on the part of outsiders, which presumably made them unwilling to cooperate with penal institutions.

In my main interview with the same governor, he elaborated on his feeling of poor integration with the outside world. In particular, he discussed the possible reasons for the isolation he felt so strongly. For one thing, he claimed that the prison system might be at fault, being resistant to feelers from outside organizations. Secondly, he repeated what he had said earlier: that outsiders often seem to be frightened by the prison system, and therefore shun it. Thirdly, and related to the second point, he claimed that other agencies involved in rehabilitation prefer to stay away from criminals, leaving their treatment to the prison system alone. He vacillated between these various reasons for the alleged isolation:

> [It's my] impression that the prison system is disregarded; it's so disregarded. We [the prison system] are such a compact unit that they feel they cannot penetrate into us. . . . [I guess my view of this derives] from many, many hundreds of impressions you get when you read the daily newspapers, etc. I have the feeling that those who deal with pure social work don't [want to have anything to do with us]. God knows—perhaps they are afraid of us, because various social institutions around the country prefer not to deal with criminals. When a criminal arrives in [the prison system, that's where he stays].

Though the governor seemed uncertain about the relative blame of the prison system and external organizations, he ended up where he had spontaneously started, by placing primary emphasis on the unwillingness of others to penetrate seriously into the prison system. After arguing that members of the courts and of the Prosecuting Authority seldom communicate directly with prison staff members despite the fact that they are responsible for sending offenders to prison, he exclaimed with great vigor:

> Contact with these organizations—it's not just a matter of efficiency, but also that you want others to be a little interested in what you are doing. To work in a prison can be a terribly lonely job. An accusation that can be made against society in general is that people know far too little about prison life. . . . A single visit is not enough in order really to understand what goes on in a prison; you have to . . . be there for a long while.

To this governor, the alleged unwillingness of others to try to understand what goes on inside a prison shaded off into a tendency on their part to look down on prison personnel:

> What I have said about the attitude of society affects lower-level staff members most directly; we [senior staff members] can bite a little and [answer back]. When many of [the lower-level staff members] dislike to talk about the fact that they are employed in the prison system—well, this is the reason: . . . they prefer to remain anonymous because they feel that their work is not valued.

The governor of *Maximum Security* also claimed that the prison system exists in isolation from the outside community, but he expressed his view with less vehemence, and without implying that isolation was such a major problem for his institution. In my first conversation with him he said, somewhat jokingly, that my study would probably verify the hypothesis I no doubt had in mind, namely that a prison does not have very many contacts outside the prison system. In my interview with him he elaborated on this, in words reminiscent of those used by the governor of *Medium Security,* but without the same forcefulness:

> We could wish that others would show a greater interest in what we are doing with the prisoners; people who are really interested in problems of resocialization [ought to be interested in what we are doing as well] . . . . It's human that they wash their hands [and just send the case on to us] ; this is the reason why there are so few connections. The other links are uninterested.

The governors specified the general isolation of penal institutions to relations with *"social institutions," the courts, the Prosecuting Authority,* and (at least by implication) *the police.* The courts and the Prosecuting Authority were mentioned by both governors; one also mentioned "social institutions" and the other the police. By "social institutions" the governor in question seemed to mean certain organizations doing "pure social work": state and municipal welfare agencies, hospitals, and specialized treatment institutions. When referring to the police, the other governor primarily thought of the local Criminal Police Division. As we shall see later, however, other staff members did have fairly frequent direct communication with welfare agencies, hospitals, other treatment institutions, and the police. And the staff members responsible for communications with these organizations were in part rather satisfied with their external relations.

The above-mentioned comments suggest that staff members tend to view as satisfactory those communications on which they specialize. Further data, to be presented below, indicate a similar tendency. But in order to warn against exaggerating and "perfecting" such a finding, let me repeat that both governors were *dissatisfied and more or less responsible for* communication with the courts[5] and the Prosecuting Authority. By way of conclusion to our discussion of the governors' external communications, two alleged consequences of the lack of communication with the courts and the Prosecuting Authority may be mentioned. In the first place, due to an unwillingness or inability to communicate, members of these organizations are presumably quite ignorant of the content of the sanctions they are imposing.

> They [the Prosecuting Authority] have an extremely unclear picture of what preventive measures consist of, and they ought to know [more about it] because they are the ones who demand preventive measures; and the judges ought to know more too, because they are the ones who decide. This is a tremendous weakness.[6]

Secondly, the alleged lack of communication is claimed to cause misunderstanding between the parties involved, thus impeding the work of the prison staff.

> It's strange that [the relationship with] the courts and the Prosecuting Authority is so distant. And the consequence of it is clear: when a man [i.e., an offender] comes here, he has heard about things like "half time," "prison year"—they have told him an awful lot about that. And that's wrong; that's poor cooperation, and we are unable to do anything about it.

"Half time" refers to release on parole after half of the prison sentence has been served (at the time of study, this could be granted by the Prison Bureau only to inmates serving a sentence of three years or more), and "prison year" refers to the notion that due to regular release on parole, a year in prison is actually less than twelve months. Staff members feel that release on parole is not and should not be "automatic," but that inmates are told that it is automatic by representatives of the courts and the Prosecuting Authority. Inducing such misunderstandings in the inmate allegedly causes difficulties in handling him in the institution.

Before proceeding to a discussion of the ministers' communication, a few words should be said about the assistant governor (in *Maximum Security* only). The assistant governor had had wide experience in correctional work. However, when I interviewed him for the present study, he had barely spent four months in his job as assistant governor, coming directly from the Prison Bureau.

To a large extent, the role of the assistant governor is an "internal" one. He is more or less supreme head of the general "treatment" program, including some of the leisure time activities. Those directly responsible for carrying out the various aspects of the program report to him. However, the assistant governor is also to some degree responsible for communication with the Prison Bureau, especially in regard to complaints and certain applications from inmates. Two points should be noted concerning the assistant governor's communication with the Bureau. First, he described the communication in question in terms indicating a lower degree of informality and personalization than was characteristic of the governor's relations. For example, he volunteered the information that when Bureau people visited the institution, they would seldom talk with him. Secondly, though not directly dissatisfied with his communication with the Bureau, he did restrain his enthusiasm. In part he did so in subtle ways, by casually commenting that though he knew the people in the Bureau very well due to his years as a staff member there, "you don't always think as [they do] when you start working in an institution." Furthermore, answering my question of whether or not he would like more contact with outside organizations (Appendix II, question 11), he stated:

> Yes, possibly with the Prison Bureau. . . . I regard it as a good thing when people there call and want to get something explained. And I am interested in maintaining and strengthening that contact, because we are dealing with the same cases, on different levels. . . . But by saying such a thing [i.e., that communication could be strengthened], one implies that it isn't so strong now, and I don't mean that. . . . Communication is excellent, but it should be *broadened.*

The assistant governor's ambivalence concerning communication with the Bureau constitutes a bleak forerunner of the strongly negative views of other staff members.

The minister and the social workers are responsible for direct communication with a number of external organizations, and to some extent they share roles as specialists. I shall first discuss the direct communications of the minister.

Realms of specialization in external communication

The importance of the minister as a direct external communicator is especially clear in relation to a number of private organizations. Of particular significance are religious charitable organizations such as the Salvation Army and Inner Mission societies, as well as a large number of non-religious private organizations, such as the Red Cross, youth clubs, teachers' colleges, and some commercial organizations. Above all, the minister communicates with these organizations in an attempt to bring to his institution people interested in contributing to leisure time and "cultural" activities. In *Medium Security*, the minister is also responsible for setting up the regular educational program, having contacts with the organizations referred to here in this capacity as well.

Again it is extremely difficult to give precise indications of frequency of direct external communication. One of the ministers interviewed for this study stressed that frequency varies, being higher at certain times of the year than at others. He stressed that the beginning of a semester is always particularly crowded with contacts, because programs are being lined up. He estimated the number of contacts with private organizations by letter, telephone, or in face-to-face contexts as twenty during the month of September (the beginning of the fall semester). According to this minister, contact is sought from the outside as well as from the inside, but he did stress initiation from the inside as more frequent.

A minister is also responsible to some degree for direct communication with state and municipal treatment institutions, such as institutions for alcoholics and drug addicts.

However, other staff members, notably psychiatrists and social workers, are more clearly specialists in this sphere. Furthermore, the ministers claimed that the frequency of their direct communication with these organizations is far lower than with private organizations. As one minister put it:

> Then we have contact with institutions managed by the state, [such as] X [an institution for alcoholics] and Y [an institution for drug addicts]. Here there are contacts of all kinds. . . . [But] there is most communication with private organizations, there is no doubt about that; private organizations are more directed toward resocialization [of criminals], while state-run institutions are more oriented toward extreme cases.

Communication with other major sets of outside organizations is even more clearly handled by other staff members.

More specifically, what are the content and form of the ministers' direct communications with private organizations? Content has been touched on already, but requires more extended treatment. As earlier, the content and form of direct external communication are most easily discussed together.

Content and form of communication

To some degree, the ministers' communication with the private organizations referred to above is formalized and depersonalized: they are officially required to communicate directly with the organizations in question, and their communications appear in some measure to be geared to the organizations as whole bodies. Such communication generally is in writing. This is only a minor part of the picture, however: to a large degree, the ministers also have informal and personal communication with private organizations. Such communication is almost always oral, and more often by telephone than in face-to-face contexts.

> There are all sorts of contacts, from telephones—first of all in writing the first time we seek contact, but very often over the telephone afterwards, and that's reciprocal.

This does not mean, however, that face-to-face contact is absent. Both of the ministers interviewed for this study actively sought face-to-face contact with members of outside organizations. They were constantly traveling, giving lectures and speeches, trying to bring outsiders to the institutions by talking personally to them. Both appeared to be of the opinion that personal contacts are more efficient than impersonal ones, and that personalized communication can best be accomplished in face-to-face settings.

> I believe in being together, and when we were at that meeting, all of us, our contact was extremely good. . . . We have tried to pull [others] in . . . by giving them especially hearty invitations to meetings and so on, to pull them into our activities, and sort of get them to participate. (Paraphrased from interview notes taken after the interview.)

In terms of content, the ministers' communication with private organizations is, as indicated already, primarily focused on providing the institution with leisure-time and educational programs. But both ministers considered such programs only as a means to a much more important end. Both showed a strong interest in providing programs which would ensure *"contact" between the incarcerated inmate and the community outside*; programs which would "bridge the gap" between the inmate and the world. They saw inmate "contact" with the community as exceedingly valuable, and as having two interrelated consequences.

First, they assumed that the establishment of such contact would give the inmate a more realistic understanding of and positive view toward the outside community. Secondly, they felt that representatives of the community would be given a more intimate understanding of the problems of the inmate. The following excerpt illustrates both of the alleged consequences. The respondent started in general and rather melodramatic terms, but after a while became more specific:

The human contact between the inmate and the world in general is extremely important. . . . And we have to use all the openings we have, all of the possibilities; we have to establish . . . bridgeheads outside. . . . Well, the word *bridgehead* is of course taken from the military, and of course it means that you have set foot in an enemy country; but, well, the world outside the prison walls isn't exactly enemy country, but it is at least a foreign country, and it is also a country where you can be exposed to gunfire, and then it's important to have footholds or bridgeheads in the foreign country. [For example], the prison visitor service arranged through the Red Cross, it doesn't only operate so that the inmate in his cell receives a visit from the outside; it also operates so that those out there gain an impression of the inmate, and they can even help him later with regard to finding work and supporting him when the chips are down. . . . So this is a two-way process. (Paraphrased from notes taken after the interview.)

General view of communications with private organizations

What can be said, in summary form, about the ministers' degree of satisfaction with their direct communications with private organizations?

Both ministers claimed that more frequent and deeper communications with certain private organizations would be useful for their purposes. As one of them expressed it:

I should like to have more contact, above all with those institutions which have people who have been in rough weather and who have managed [i.e., criminals, alcoholics, etc., who have later turned to conventional life]. . . . Alcoholics Anonymous, for example. . . . For example X, he has stayed clear of trouble for a number of years now, and he is one who can help out with religious services here. Those contacts, they are the best, above all because they understand the problems involved. Others often don't understand what's really going on, and some of them create more distance than contact.

But as the excerpt suggests, the minister in question referred to a need for better communication with rather rare and specialized organizations. The ministers generally claimed to be in satisfactory communication with "regular" private organizations: the Salvation Army, Inner Mission societies, non-religious charitable organizations, various economic enterprises, etc. For example, the ministers viewed the private charitable organizations as

> ... established as a network around us ... and we have lots of contact with them; in fact, they are our saviors ... but these are established precisely to be the bridge between the prison and society. ... So you have to say there is contact, certainly. But let me emphasize that these are the voluntary ones.

As with the governors, it is possible that the ministers' roles as communication specialists, in their case with private organizations, made them present their direct communications in a more favorable light than their feelings actually warranted. Again, no test of this possibility exists. But again, and though the reader may not be entirely satisfied with the evidence, my extensive association with these men—especially in one of the institutions—and the sense of honesty and openness they gave me, does not support this as a major explanation.

View of communication with other organizations

What about the ministers' views of communications with organizations in relation to which they are less clearly, or not at all, communication specialists? State and municipal treatment organizations and organizations within the prison system are considered particularly relevant by the ministers, because they impinge directly on their attempts to "bridge" the gap between the inmate and society.

The ministers' general satisfaction with their relative lack of direct access to state and municipal treatment institutions (on which social workers and psychiatrists are specialists) is clearly fairly low. It should be noted, however, that their dissatisfaction did not appear to be quite as pronounced as that of one governor, who worried greatly about his lack of access to "social institutions" (see above). Interestingly, though neither minister nor governor is a clear communication specialist in relation to official treatment organizations, the governor is even less of a specialist in this realm than is the minister.

While the ministers expressed moderate discontent with lack of direct access to official treatment organizations, they voiced deep worry and dissatisfaction over lack of direct access to organizations inside the prison system. To both ministers, their personal lack of direct access to organizations within the prison system shaded off into a lack of communication on the part of the individual institution as a whole—this despite the fact that certain colleagues did have extensive contact. In sharp contrast to the communication specialists, who viewed their direct communication with other organizations inside the prison system as very satisfactory (see the preceding discussion of the governors), the ministers viewed the prison system as more or less atomized.

Above all, both ministers found communication with the Prison Bureau to be totally inadequate. The minister in the treatment-oriented institution was particularly vehement about it. In more detail: In my first interview with him, the minister in *Medium Security* told me that he was greatly interested in expanding the use of furloughs and passes for inmates, but that the Prison Bureau was against it. He claimed that the unwillingness of the Bureau to relax its rules concerning furloughs and passes (see Appendix I) was directly related to a lack of communication between the Bureau and the institution. He seemed to imply that if communication had been adequate, the Bureau would have "understood" and consented to a demand for an increased use of furloughs and passes. At this point in our conversation, the minister became agitated, several times striking his fist on the table to stress his points. Toward the end of the interview, he grabbed a list of names of employees in the Prison Bureau, and claimed with great vigor that though he had met the Prison Director a few times, he had not even seen, let alone met, any of the other employees in the Bureau. He rapidly read off a number of names on the list, for each name exclaiming that he had no idea at all who the person was. His list was a bit out of date, and it may be significant that several of the people he specifically mentioned as total strangers working in the Bureau, had actually left the Bureau for other jobs.

In a later interview, the same minister discussed his views of communication between the Bureau and the institution in more detail. Two points may be singled out.

In the first place, he claimed that *communication from the institution to the Bureau* was poor to the point of exasperation; that it was impossible to get anything "across" to the final decision-makers. In this connection, he employed two expressions which, as we shall see, are in general use among senior staff members other than the governors. The Bureau, he claimed, is constantly engaged in "distant control" of the institution and of the minister's work, in the sense that the Bureau members "just read the documents" when making decisions concerning release on parole, furloughs, and the like. In other words, he blamed the inadequacy of communication from the institution to the Bureau on the Bureau: the Bureau allegedly withdraws from anything but formal and depersonalized channels of communication, which, he claimed, are totally ineffective since a series of very relevant "facts" cannot be communicated this way. According to the minister and to many other staff members, the facts in question add up to an intuitive grasp of the total situation of the inmate, whose "fate" is being decided. It is claimed that such a grasp of the total situation, presumably necessary as a basis for sensible decision-making, must be transmitted informally: swiftly, without delay, whenever needed. Likewise, it is felt that the grasp of the situation cannot be transmitted to an organization as a body: it has to be brought across to another concrete individual.

In the second place, the minister in question claimed that informal and person *communication from the Bureau to the institution* was totally inadequate. Thus, when an inmate is refused release on parole

> ... he just receives the refusal, [and no reason is given]. He just gets that darned refusal, without even an explanation to the council here. ... We ought to be in a position to decide whether the explanation [should go on to the inmate].

Note that the governors do apparently at times receive explanation (see last quote on p. 44). The explanations do not seem to be passed on to others.

In short, the minister in the treatment-oriented institution felt strongly that informal and personal communication with the Prison Bureau was inadequate or lacking completely. The minister in the maximum-security prison appeared to feel exactly the same way about it, but he expressed it somewhat less emphatically. To him, lack of informal and personal communication resulted in a general lack of (diffusely defined) "cooperation."

Both ministers also claimed that their lack of direct access to other penal institutions—prisons and specialized penal establishments—was a very great problem. They felt a lack of informal and personalized communication to be particularly aggravating. As earlier, the minister in the treatment-oriented institution was most vehement about it. He expressed it in the following terms:

> I have tried to start cooperating with the other prison ministers, but it is [impossible]. I have written a letter to the two other prison ministers in [the capital city], and I have sent a copy to the bishop, and in this letter I have stressed that there are many ministers working in prisons, and no mechanism for joint activity. ... This is a one-man show. And it turns out that this is an important problem for us, and it's also the case for the social

workers, the occupational therapists, etc. We don't have external contacts, and we don't look beyond our own noses. . . . It's *personal* contact that's lacking to a considerable extent. I think it would have been a gain if we could meet now and then, and the same for the inspectors, the social workers and the work supervisors . . . and the medical sector. . . . Now we just learn from *the inmate* what conditions are like in other institutions.

The respondent did not offer any explanation of the ministers' inability to communicate directly. Neither did he explain why the governor and other staff members, as communication specialists, represented an information link poorer than the inmates.

THE SOCIAL WORKERS

Realms of specialization in external communication

In penal institutions in the Scandinavian country concerned, social workers rank at least as high as governors and ministers in having boundary responsibilities. In fact, the social workers I interviewed may have considered themselves more significant than other staff members in this respect. An external orientation on the part of social workers follows from the nature of their work. Their major ultimate task is that of helping the inmate to "readjust" to the outside community, by finding housing facilities and occupational possibilities for him, and by participating in supervising him. Their readjustment efforts are probably often perceived by the inmate as additional measures of control. But in any case, their efforts do lead them to extensive communication with outside organizations. Four major areas of direct external communication should be stressed.

In the first place, the importance of the social workers as direct external communicators is very clear in relation to various private charitable organizations, especially branches of the Salvation Army, the Inner Mission Society, and the

Red Cross. All three organizations have half-way houses in or near the capital city, where inmates released on parole or on milder preventive measures may be placed for shorter or longer periods of time. The social worker's role as specialist in relation to charitable organizations is shared by the minister (though as we shall see, social worker and minister differ in terms of communication content).

Secondly, the social workers are specialists in communicating with representatives of a number of private commercial enterprises. The communication primarily concerns employment for released inmates. Again, the social workers share the role of specialist with the ministers.

Thirdly, the social workers are clearly specialists on direct communication with the major "semi-official" organization in the institutional environment: the National Welfare Association and its various subordinate welfare offices. (This is an association of local welfare offices working for the prevention of crime, especially as probation and parole agencies. Strictly speaking it is a private organization, but it receives a substantial proportion of its funds from the national government. For details, see Appendix I.) The welfare office in the capital city has a small half-way house where released inmates may be placed. Welfare officers throughout the country are generally responsible for supervising inmates released on parole. This gives the social workers in the institutions a reason for communicating with the organizations in question, especially when supervisory relationships are first established.

Finally, the social workers are specialists on direct communication with several fully official organizations: the police, including the Prosecuting Authority (partly shared with others), the municipal social boards (granting "social aid," often of a financial kind, to those who are considered to need it), the Ministry of Social Affairs, the Ministry of Justice (departments other than the Prison Bureau), certain staff members in other prisons, and to some degree outside treatment institutions, such as mental hospitals. Note, however, that in the latter two realms other staff members—the governor and the psychiatrists respectively—are equally important.

Again, it is extremely difficult to provide exact frequencies of external communication. But when associating with these men and women (which I did for a number of weeks because I had my main headquarters in their offices),[7] I was struck by the sense of urgency which they seemed to attach to their boundary activities. If this urgency constituted nothing but an artificial reaction to the presence of an outside observer, the social workers in question must have been the most proficient of actors. Even more than other staff members, they seemed to attach great emotional significance to their external relations, and to consider the relations vital for their institution as a whole. They behaved and talked as if they viewed their institution as a kind of organism, whose continual contractions had a dangerous tendency to close pores vital to survival. The sense of urgency was especially pronounced in *Medium Security*, the treatment-oriented institution.

Apparently, I am not alone in having sensed such an urgency. Several of the social workers were referred to by other staff members, and by representatives of outside organizations, as extremely persistent and arduous laborers in the field of external relations. While generally unsuccessful in their efforts to "readjust" inmates, and while probably using tragically inefficient means, at least they cannot be accused of not trying.

Content and form of communication

The social workers' direct communication with outside organizations is informalized and personalized in the extreme. The content of the communication covers a wide span of activity; social workers are to a great extent jacks of all external trades.

Form and content may be discussed in relation to the four

major classes of external organizations mentioned above. Note that the content of the direct communications to be described here in part explicitly involves the establishment of indirect communications. In so far as this is the case, indirect communications also have to be discussed.

1. *Communication with private charitable organizations.* The informal and personal character of direct communication is easily seen in relation to charitable organizations. The social workers contact superintendents of private half-way houses on the spur of the moment, whenever needed, and not according to prearranged rules. They know the half-way house superintendents personally and very well. The informal and personal character of communication is expressed over the telephone or in face-to-face talks. The major content of communication with representatives of a half-way house consists of arranging the details of release on parole or on milder preventive measures. "Arranging the details of release" may be further subdivided into four areas of activity, constituting the total sequence of a release to a half-way house.[8]

First, a release to a half-way house requires that the superintendent of the half-way house be willing to receive the inmate in question. While some half-way houses have few or no rules restricting admittance, others do have some restricting regulations, and almost all have long waiting lists. The social worker from the institution has to contend with these circumstances, and to convince the superintendent or his representative that the inmate is worth receiving.

Second, a release to a half-way house necessitates, as does any other release, the involvement and cooperation of a number of other organizations. The social worker may obtain cooperation with other organizations through his informal and personal relations with half-way house superintendents. Being representatives of private, charitable, and therefore presumably "neutral" organizations, the latter at times have the confidence even of representatives of official organizations, such as the Prison Bureau. If the institution social worker has managed to make him interested, a superintendent of a half-way house may play the role of mediating link with the Bureau. As one half-way house superintendent described it:

> Personally I have a good deal of contact with the Prison Bureau, because many of my men here are released on parole, and I have bothered X, Y and Z [in the Bureau] quite a bit through the years. . . . I meet with them personally first, and then I write about it. . . . In a person-to-person discussion we look at the documents, and then we usually agree that I write something about it. . . . In most cases it's about men I have had contact with. Something is going to happen—for example, an inmate has applied for release on parole but the Bureau takes a dim view of it, and when you know the inmate personally from prior experience, you can argue with them. . . . These are things that a social worker in a prison can't do; they don't have the authority to do it, they are not supposed to mess up the governor's communications . . . they are so restricted by the regulations and so on, . . . but I can do such things as an outsider, and often social workers call me and say "can't you talk to them about it." . . . It wouldn't look good if a social worker in the prison contacted the Bureau. . . . Impossible to say how often [I do this] ; during one month I can bother them three or four times, and then months can pass. . . . [But] when you have good connections, you have to be careful and not abuse them, and if you don't have a first-rate plan [for the inmate, you might as well forget about it]. And questions about furloughs also arise. . . . Mind you, the institution doesn't ask me to contact the Bureau; it's the individual social worker who asks . . . he says "can't you drop in and ask them."

Note how the superintendent quoted here implied that he had to be very selective when indirectly helping the social workers. A plan had to be first-rate for the superintendent to take it to the Bureau. Furthermore, not all superintendents of half-way houses seem to have the full confidence of the Prison Bureau. To gain such confidence seems to take wide experience with offenders, so that the individual superintendent clearly gives the impression of "knowing what he is talking about." It may also require a personality giving the impression of trustworthiness. It should also be mentioned that when communicating with representatives of official organizations, the half-way house people not only work *for* the institution social workers, they also use their "connections" to correct the picture of the inmate which they have received through the institution social workers. In short, overt support of the social workers may be combined with a covert double-checking of them. As one half-way house superintendent expressed the latter function:

> X [in the Bureau] is a member of our board, and we have telephone contact, and he is here on board meetings. . . . Well, for example, we received an application from WA [a penal institution], and then I wanted a little more information, and then I called X and asked him to look into it for me. This is only X, and he is a big shot there, so then we don't need any contact with others in the Prison Bureau.

Third, release to a half-way house involves the actual sending of the inmate to the half-way house in question. If taken seriously, this is in itself no little task, and implies considerable communication with representatives of the half-way house. Usually, the social worker personally brings the inmate to the institution, trying to acquaint him with the superintendent and the rest of the staff.

Finally, release on parole often results in reincarceration. This also implies informal and personal communication with staff members of the half-way house. Personal belongings have to be brought back to the institution, and the task of fetching them is trivial but tragic. More significantly, the reincarceration of an inmate may disrupt the relationship between the institution and the half-way house, and the social workers probably see it as important to cement the relationship for future use. The difficulty of this task seems to vary. Though my data on this point are impressionistic, the most important problem appears to be that of solving the question of blame in a manner satisfactory from the point of view of the half-way house. On the one hand, the half-way house superintendent may have to be convinced that the penal institution did not make a serious mistake in releasing the inmate; that the institution is fully reliable. On the other hand, the half-way house superintendent may have to be assured that the prison people do not blame the half-way house for what happened. In cases where penal institution as well as half-way house have to be relieved of blame to ensure continued co-operation, blame is probably placed on the inmate. Thus, in order to help inmates in the future, social workers may have to make particular inmates appear exceptionally unworthy of help.

2. *Communication with private commercial organizations.* When communicating with representatives of half-way houses, the social worker to some degree has to contend with grudging, unwilling and opposing forces. This, however, is doubly so in his dealings with representatives of private commercial enterprises, whom he contacts to find employment for inmates. The suspicions of half-way house representatives, who want their institutions to be orderly and of good reputation, are rather latent, implicit, and between the lines. The suspicions of representatives of private firms, who are not in any way committed to the general cause of "combating crime," are manifest, explicit, and often stated in so many words.

Release on parole as well as on milder preventive measures generally requires that the inmate has a job waiting for him. However, rules vary concerning the question of whether the employer must be notified of the inmate's criminal background. Release on regular parole (from *Maximum Security*) does not require that the employer be informed of the inmate's record, while release on milder preventive measures (from *Medium Security*) does.[9] Because of this difference, social workers in the two institutions have somewhat different relations with potential employers.

The social workers in *Maximum Security* can, and often do, minimize their direct contact with employers, leaving much of the direct communication to the inmate himself. Of course, the inmate rarely indicates his criminal background to the employer. The non-participation of the social worker varies in degree. In some cases, he stays completely out of touch with the employer, on the ground that:

> When we call from here we *have* to say who is calling. It's much better that the inmate himself answers ads in the newspapers, and then we can arrange for a pass for him [to talk to the employer]. In this respect we try to accommodate the inmate as far as we can.

In other cases, the social worker lets the inmate make the first contact with the employer, and then tries to cement the relationship by operating in disguise on the sidelines. To operate "in disguise" involves prodding the inmate on, giving him advice, and even helping him to see the employer, all the time without entering direct negotiations as a social worker with the employer. This way the social worker does not have to reveal the inmate's background. One of the social workers described her operations in disguise in the following terms:

> [We contact the employer directly only] in those cases where the inmate wants us to; we don't do so without his wanting us to. [We usually tell the inmate that he ought to put all the cards on the table, for his own sake.] To a large extent we arrange a pass for him, [we drive him down] and then we wait discreetly in the background. I am usually "the aunt who owns the car."

Of course, in some cases the social workers in *Maximum Security* do participate fully, communicating directly with the potential employer. In the treatment-oriented institution they apparently always do so, since they are required to inform the employer of the inmate's criminal background.

When a social worker communicates directly, he tries to make the communication as informal and personal as possible. He attempts to establish steady relationships with particular individuals, usually through conversations, feeling that they best ensure informality and personable relations. As one social worker described it:

> I have completely stopped counting on the Communal Labor Office, so in fact we have to find jobs for these people ourselves. Now, I have some permanent contacts [i.e., employers] where I can put all of the cards on the table. And we mustn't abuse those. In other cases, we use the newspapers, and we call and ask if there is a vacancy, and if there is, I put the cards on the table. And then you sort of understand fast: if they ask too many questions I usually break off, and if they are sort of in doubt, I usually don't prod further. But then you can suddenly have some nice surprises, too. . . . [I use my telephone all day long.]

The expression "to put the cards on the table" was used frequently by the social workers. To them, it seemed to symbolize the practical difficulties following from having to be honest: being open about the criminal background of inmates is to a large extent a gamble. It is precisely the atmosphere of gambling which, in the eyes of the social workers, makes informal and personalized relations necessary. As they see it, almost invariably the chips would already be down if communication were formal and impersonal; only by informality and personalized relations did they feel they had a chance to persuade and commit a potential employer. As one of the social workers tried to express the point:

> If you're going to get things rolling, you have to . . . have "the feel of things," or what should I call it. There are no special rules for the social sector, only those that are relevant for the staff as a whole. . . . You have to be quite a diplomat, because you are selling second-rate merchandise, and at the same time we mustn't hide anything; we always put the cards on the table.

In both institutions, the social workers are required to help inmates find a place to live. Communication with landlords will not be discussed in detail, since it does not involve relations with other organizations. Suffice it to say that rules as well as methods are similar to those relevant for communications with potential employers.

3. *Communication with a semi-official organization.* When communicating with members of the National Welfare Association and its subordinate welfare offices, the social workers feel more on home ground. Several of the employees in the various local offices are social workers by training, and all have "social work" in a vague and general sense of the word as a primary goal.

A brief review of the formal structure of the National Welfare Association and its subdivisions may be found in Appendix I. The social workers are institution specialists on direct communication with members of this semi-official organization. Again, two familiar themes appear: communication is to a large extent informal and personalized. Communication is established swiftly, on the spur of the moment, according to need rather than rules, and geared to particular individuals rather than to the organization or its sub-units as abstract collectivities. "Connections" are developed and maintained by oral means: by telephone or in face-to-face encounters. In addition, "connections" are established through meetings in a special voluntary association for social workers employed in the prison system or as welfare officers. At the meetings in this association, informal papers on topics concerning parole are usually presented. At times, weekend meetings are arranged outside the capital city to debate topics of general criminological interest.

All of the social workers in the institutions expressed a high degree of satisfaction concerning their communications with welfare officers. There is little reason to doubt that they expressed their genuine feeling. I knew several of the respondents intimately; furthermore, it would have been easy for them to blame any lack of adequate communication on others (such as the welfare officers) rather than on themselves. However, ten welfare officers in the local welfare office interviewed for this study apparently viewed the matter differently, expressing varying degrees of dissatisfaction.

They indicated that they had extensive informal and personalized communication with the institution social workers (in addition to receiving, by regulation, certain written documents on the inmates), thus providing independent corroboration of the social workers' statements about communication form. They also indicated that they did communicate very well with the social workers *as such*. They appeared to feel, however, that the social workers constituted an inadequate link with others in the prison system, especially other senior staff members. In a word, they seemed to feel that they did not quite "get through" to the prison staff as a whole.

By now the reader will have noticed that the staff members' views of the adequacy of communication in general with given outside organizations is characterized by a lack of consensus. By referring to a similar (probably uncommunicated) disagreement between the institution social worker and the outside welfare officers, the lack of consensus is widened to include outsiders as well.

Since the welfare officers' negative feeling specifically focuses on the degree to which social workers seem to inform other prison employees of boundary activities and relations, a few further comments are in order. Essentially, the welfare officers complained that communication with penal institutions is inadequate in two overlapping and related respects.

In the first place, several officers claimed that prison employees other than the social workers are at times uninformed and unappreciative concerning the sheer difficulties involved in supervising parolees. Presumably, the prison people expect too much of the welfare officers.

> [We do perhaps lack something] when it comes to the imagination of the prison system. [They don't understand] how an apparently kind man is on the outside. . . . A man can be quite different on the outside; they [the senior staff in prisons] can be

pretty ignorant concerning how a man is outside. They say *he* must be tried on parole, because he behaves so well. There ought perhaps to be a little more information on both sides.

This ties in with a feeling that prison employees other than social workers do not fully appreciate the general importance of the work performed by the various welfare offices.

It has happened that a governor has casually said [to an inmate], "well, drop in at the welfare office when you find the time for it." . . . I don't mean to say that reporting at the office is all there is to a [supervisory relationship], but at least they have to be told very clearly that they *have* to report here. I don't think stories like this just are something that the clients have invented.

In the above quote, the welfare officer in question inadvertently admitted that welfare officers at times rely on information received through the released inmate. Welfare officers certainly accused the prison staff of doing the same:

We always take what the clients say about prisons with a grain of salt, but the prison people tend to be a little too uncritical in swallowing what they say about us.

The feeling that "prison people" do not appreciate the difficulties and importance of outside work, expressed in their alleged tendency to rely uncritically on inmate information, is claimed to complicate the work of the welfare officers. This leads to the second sense in which welfare officers find communication with penal institutions inadequate. The welfare officers feel that, owing to lack of informational exchange, the work done for the inmate by the penal institution and the welfare office is insufficiently integrated. The prison system is largely blamed for this.

I think we [i.e., the welfare office] should start much earlier, right after the sentence is passed, and try to find a job for the inmate and plan [ahead]. And not like it is now: I get a telephone call two days before release, because they [the prison staff] receive the final word from the Prison Bureau [so late]. I realize it's terribly difficult for the institution people, [but] the way in which it is prepared is certainly not satisfactory. [The inmate] is sort of like a ball which is thrown back and forth; the prison does its job and [then washes its hands of the whole affair], and if something goes wrong later, it's our fault. This kind of thing is strange; that attitude goes deep ... we ought to cooperate from the start in order to get something done. .... Now everyone sits in his own little box and knows only what is going on there, and that's not enough, at least with regard to juvenile delinquents, I should think.

To some extent a lack of integration may be explained by a fear on the part of prison personnel of giving unco-opted strangers—the welfare officers—increased information about the secrets of prison life. Though this was never stated by anyone, at least one welfare officer came very close to suggesting it by saying:

It has always been a rule that the welfare officer visits the prison [a particular institution not included in this study] once a week, and I think that ought to be increased. The governor up there wants a permanent, full-time social worker who stays up there [he does not want to expand our visits, and I disagree with that]. ... I don't mean to say that there is poor cooperation, but the governor thinks it's best for him to have his own social worker. ... I am uncertain about that; the inmates *like* to see someone from the outside.

However, most likely we are faced with a two-sided issue: lack of integration is probably also in considerable measure related to the welfare officers' fear of being run and co-opted by members of the prison system. This, in any case, is an important consideration on the part of those welfare officers who are wary of full official attachment of the welfare association to the penal system. As indicated in Appendix I, the semi-detached status of the welfare association is currently a debated topic in the organization. Some feel that full formal status as a state organization would alleviate the two types of communication problems outlined here, while others suspect that the welfare organization would be co-opted.

The welfare officers' fear of being co-opted, which in a sense is inconsistent with their wish for further information, no doubt makes it necessary for prison social workers to labor for their communications even in this sphere.

4. *Communication with official organizations.* As indicated already, the relevant official organizations include the police, the municipal social boards, the Ministry of Justice (departments other than the Prison Bureau), the Ministry of Social Affairs, other prisons, and treatment organizations of various sorts.

The social workers summarized the content of their communication with these organizations by using the two common-sense terms "straightening things out" and "getting particulars." In more detail: The social workers feel that when inmates are incarcerated, a number of daily-life affairs are left unattended. Furthermore, they feel that inmates are less prone than other people to lead an orderly life on the outside. They also claim that a number of unexpected events take place in inmates' outside environment that have to be acted upon, often on short notice. They consider (perhaps a bit reluctantly) "straightening such things out," i.e., reorganizing them into a more stable pattern, as an important part of "social work." "Getting particulars" implies cross-checking data received from the inmate, his relatives, his prior employers, etc., as well as obtaining new details concerning the inmate and his situation outside. Very often, the information is intended for the social worker's (or the psychiatrist's) recommendation for or against release on parole, and thereby as a basis for the council's recommendation to the Prison Bureau.

The reorganizational and cross-checking functions are, of course, often combined when social workers communicate with official organizations. The illustrative incident described at the beginning of this chapter is an example of this. Here it is described in the social worker's own words:

I have a man who has been given temporary release now. He is from X city. His wife was here and visited him on Wednesday, then on her way home she drove off the road and broke her jaw. [The inmate's lawyer called and told us about it.] Then I called the hospital to see how she [actually] was, and I called the social board to hear how their [little boy] was, and then I called the local police [to hear their opinion about a welfare furlough in order for him to take care of things]. I did *not* call the chief of police [and I was blamed for that]. Then I talked for an hour and a half with the governor [over the telephone; by now it was Saturday night], to press him [to grant a welfare furlough in view of the circumstances]. When I had all of this information I had something to clinch the argument with the governor, because he asks *why?* And then I worked through the whole thing again the other way around, and then he got his furlough at 10:30 Saturday night. So you see, it doesn't work if you come empty-handed in the council; an application has no effect then.

Nowhere is the informal character of direct external communications seen more clearly. Though almost all staff members claimed there were few or no specific rules or regulations guiding their communications (Appendix II, question 7), the social workers appeared particularly vehement about it, and included relations to official organizations. They stressed that here they had to be extremely flexible; that they had to organize the work on a day-to-day basis and according to the unique circumstances of the individual case. Though they may have exaggerated their flexibility somewhat, their description was largely corroborated by my own informal observations.

Communication with official organizations appears considerably personalized as well. Though general letters are used, telephoning to particular persons is preferred, and if the case is complex, face-to-face meetings with particular individuals are arranged. Personalized communication is considered more effective than impersonal relations.

If a case, for example, involves the Ministry of Social Affairs, usually [it can be handled by] telephone or letter. But if it is a complicated case, we go down and talk to them about it. . . . We both write letters and talk to them. . . . It depends on how complicated the case is; [sometimes] we have to try to persuade and influence people. . . . For example official rehabilitation institutions: there it's both written and oral, always both. . . . That thing is very complicated: they are not willing to take criminals; they don't just stand there with open arms . . . [and] personal contact is very important. And institutions for occupational therapy are not easy either; it's extremely difficult to place these people in schools; [you make a lot of telephone calls] and still it may not work. In two cases we have been able to place our people, and then we have had help from outside to push the case.

Often, the social workers need information of a very private nature from outsiders. In such cases, close personal contact with and knowledge of particular outside individuals seem to be considered absolutely essential. Through "personal connections," the necessary information presumably can be procured more easily, and discretion concerning the fact that the prison wants such information is guaranteed. One social worker described as follows an isolated incident where his personalized contacts apparently had not been good enough:

We need intimate details, at least in connection with applications [from inmates], because we have to verify what's in them, and then you have to be terribly careful in order not to be a bull in a china shop. I really had a story there. This inmate had told his girl friend that he was working as a sailor, while he actually was [incarcerated] here, of course. He applied for a furlough with the specific purpose of visiting a particular relative who lived outside of town, but I suspected that he was just going to visit his girl friend, and I had to find out before the council meeting. The girl worked as a nurse in X hospital, and I called the hospital, introduced myself and asked the Head Nurse if the nurse in question [the girl friend] was allowed to receive male visitors in her room. She lived there at the hospital. The Head Nurse said "of course not," and I said "thank you" and hung up. And then that Head Nurse went to the girl and said "I understand you have a boyfriend who is in prison," and the girl said "why no, he's at sea," and then the whole story came out, and the inmate was furious, of course. I called the Head Nurse and said, "How on earth could you say such a thing? It was obvious that this was between the two of us." I usually say it must be between the two of us, but I didn't in this particular case. I took it for granted. (Partly paraphrased from notes taken after the interview.)

The social workers referred to their relations with the criminal police by saying that "I have dropped surnames with all of them down there" (note the contrasting view of one of the governors); to their communications with social workers in other prisons by exclaiming that "I know all of them personally," etc. Though it is possible that the social workers may have exaggerated their own "personal connections" somewhat, their statements were largely corroborated by my informal observations: by listening to the way they talked over the telephone, how they conversed at criminological meetings, and so forth.

General view of direct communications

What can be said, in summary form, about the social workers' degree of satisfaction with their various direct communications? It seems reasonable to say that the social workers showed a certain ambivalence.

In some respects, such as in relation to potential employers and some official organizations, they felt that their communications were somewhat unsatisfactory. Phenomenologically, in these relationships they seemed to view themselves as frantically fumbling around in the dark, and as constantly bumping into an almost impenetrable wall of lack of understanding from outsiders. This feeling appeared to be more pronounced among social workers in the treatment-oriented institution than among those in the regular prison. One of the social workers tried to convey his feeling in the following words:

> Contacts could be better. The right tendency is there: we try to keep open channels going out . . . [but some] feel that the prison

system is something dangerous; some say that these [i.e., the inmates] are dangerous fellows, and we have to explain what this is all about, and even to people you should think would know better. They think [all the inmates] are here for the most terrible crimes. . . . When they hear that a man has a sentence to preventive detention, they often say no.

At the same time, the social workers expressed a fairly high degree of satisfaction with other direct communication lines, such as with the National Welfare Association, the police (note one governor's apparent dissatisfaction with lack of direct access), various official treatment institutions (note that one governor and the ministers expressed dissatisfaction with lack of direct access), and other penal institutions within the prison system (note the ministers' dissatisfaction with lack of direct access). In these relationships, the social workers seemed to view themselves as "insiders": as having intimate knowledge of the systems in question, and of where to go to find the required information.

View of communication with other organizations

What about the social workers' views on communication with organizations in relation to which they are less clearly communication specialists?

The social workers are most clearly non-specialists in relation to the Prison Bureau. In line with the ministers, they expressed dissatisfaction with their lack of direct communication with the Bureau. (Note again the contrasting view of the governors as communication specialists.) Their dissatisfaction ranged from general concern to deep worry.

In *Medium Security,* dissatisfaction was pronounced and unanimous. In strong words, the social workers there referred to the Bureau as being engaged in "distant control" of the institution and of the social workers, presumably basing its decisions on "the documents" rather than on real knowledge of the inmates. Their opinion was in accord with that of the minister in their institution (see above). The social workers in *Maximum Security,* though more often dissatisfied than not, did not voice quite as strong opinions, and were not in such full agreement. In fact, one of them claimed that he was in no way dissatisfied with his lack of direct communication with the Bureau. He explained in more detail:

> We don't have any direct relationship with the Prison Bureau, but it's my impression that the contact between the governor and the Bureau is easy; it's informal—well, it's formal, too, but—whether it's due to the governor here I don't know, but at any rate I think the informal [contact] is very good. And our road goes straight up [to the governor], and there is very good contact there, too . . . so communication is very good.

But a second social worker in *Maximum Security* claimed that her lack of direct communication with the Bureau was generally unsatisfactory, though without using strongly negative words, and the third social worker expressed his dissatisfaction in bitter tones. In short, four out of five social workers in the two institutions expressed dissatisfaction in one form or another.

THE PSYCHIATRISTS

From the description given above, a number of differences of opinion concerning communication emerge between incumbents of different roles. Arriving at the role of the prison psychiatrist, the "level of inconsistency" is stepped up still further: we also find rather sharp differences of opinion concerning form and adequacy of communication between various incumbents of one role. Inconsistencies of this kind largely cannot be found in the material on the roles of governor, minister, and social worker. With a few exceptions (such as social workers in *Maximum Security*), differences within each of these roles consist of variations in degree and vociferousness of opinion.

The differences of opinion among the psychiatrists are doubly important because the psychiatrists to a large extent believed themselves to constitute a group with high internal consensus, not only on treatment matters, but on form and adequacy of external communications as well. The belief in consensus, clearly voiced several times, appeared entirely sincere. I base this judgment on the prolonged participant-observation study referred to earlier, through which I gained intimate knowledge of two of the three psychiatrists interviewed for the present study. The belief in consensus may have functioned as a defensive reaction to a sneaking suspicion of the existence of disagreements. If so, the suspicions in question must have been unconscious. It seems more reasonable to view the unawareness of dissensus as a sign of poor communication within the so-called "team."

Realms of specialization in external communication

The importance of the psychiatrists as direct external communicators is most clearly seen in relation to various official and private treatment institutions: general and mental hospitals, the general prison hospital in the capital city, the mental hospital for insane offenders, state-run and private institutions for alcoholics (the private ones largely run by charitable organizations), psychiatric clinics, and state-run institutions for the mentally retarded. A few other organizations will be referred to as we proceed. As earlier, it is extremely hard to assess the frequency of communication. One of the psychiatrists claimed that he had some kind of contact—written or oral—with a hospital about once a month. A second psychiatrist claimed he made about three hundred telephone calls per quarter, most of them to the general hospital within the prison system. The third psychiatrist supplemented this information by saying that he had some kind of contact with one of the above-mentioned types of organizations at least once a day. Frequency of communication seemed to vary a great deal among the three psychiatrists. The psychiatrists found it very hard to say whether external communication primarily originated on the outside or on the inside.

One of the psychiatrists emphasized that he "often" gave lectures and talks to various student groups: law-students, nurses, and others. All three psychiatrists from time to time served as psychiatric expert advisers in court trials involving preventive measures (see Appendix I). All were members of and participated in a national association for psychiatrists.

Content and form of communication

With regard to content of communication, the three psychiatrists were largely in agreement. They all stressed that their communication with outside treatment institutions and with hospitals within the prison system concerned above all the transfer of inmates from their own institution to other institutions and vice versa. In addition, one of the psychiatrists served as a part-time doctor in a private institution for alcoholics. Their communication with members of the court naturally focused on their activity as psychiatric expert advisers.

With regard to form, however, the psychiatrists gave three rather widely divergent views of what was going on. One of the psychiatrists in *Medium Security* described, in a relaxed and sincere manner, how his communication with outside organizations was very informal and personalized. He implied that since mental hospitals are generally overcrowded, personal knowledge of particular doctors is necessary in order to make the hospital receive criminals as patients. He described in some detail his intimate relations with a number of particular staff members in various hospitals. He explained how he had managed to establish these relations:

> It's a great advantage that I have had contact with hospitals [and so on] as a hospital doctor myself as well as in private practice. And then I have been a medical trainee in the hospitals round

here, and therefore I know most of the doctors in the various hospitals. . . . So nothing of this is new. . . .

The psychiatrist in question had spent only two years as a prison doctor, and his various informal and personal contacts from earlier jobs were still intact. Related to this, he viewed himself

more as a psychiatrist . . . than as a prison man. . . . These paragraphs and so on: [I haven't] swallowed them yet. I am thinking of the regulations and all of those legal paragraphs. Often I have to look them up to make sure that it's correct, and that holds for others here, too.

The situation of the other psychiatrist in *Medium Security* was drastically different. He had been in the institution for fifteen years, and though trying to keep in contact with other members of his profession by participating in professional meetings and in seminars at various hospitals, he apparently felt he had to spend most of his spare time keeping abreast with criminological writings, and in participating in penological and criminological circles. Thus, while well acquainted with aspects of legal and sociological thinking about crime, he apparently tended to lose touch with developments in his own profession. In line with this, the way in which he described his communication with treatment institutions and similar organizations suggested fairly formalized and rather impersonal relations. For example, when trying to get a patient transferred to a hospital outside the prison system, it seemed that he often contacted "the hospital" rather than specific individuals working there. He tended to describe himself as an isolated man, apparently bitter about a lack of interest of the general psychiatric profession in the problems of crime.

The third psychiatrist, in *Maximum Security*, seemed to rank roughly between the other two in informality and personalization of external communication. Interestingly, his tenure in the prison system also fell, in number of years, between that of the other two psychiatrists.

General view of direct communication

What about the psychiatrists' degree of satisfaction with their various direct external communications? I mentioned above that the psychiatrists varied greatly in informality and personalization of communication. Degree of satisfaction followed suit.

The psychiatrist who showed a high degree of informality and personalization was largely satisfied with his direct communications, feeling that he received whatever information he needed and that he was able to "get across" to others whatever he wanted to tell them.

> I think the contact and the cooperation with others is as good as it ought to be. [And this also includes relations with the police.] At any rate, I don't have any difficulties—we have good cooperation there. And this includes the office of the Public Prosecutor as well; they are included in the same group.

Note here the clearly contrasting views of the two governors. To me, the psychiatrist in question appeared very sincere, as if trying to convey what he really felt about communication.

The psychiatrist who showed a low degree of informality and personalization of direct external communication, expressed himself in words strongly reminiscent of his governor's dissatisfaction with his lack of direct communication. (He was often in open conflict with the governor, however, which may indicate unawareness of consensus.) As mentioned above, the psychiatrist in question appeared bitter about a lack of interest of his professional colleagues in the problem of crime. He also felt that various treatment institutions outside the prison system were quite uncooperative; that is, unwilling to receive patients with a criminal background. He complained bitterly about his difficulties in persuading representatives of other institutions to receive his inmates. The following excerpt is in clear contrast to the excerpt quoted above:

> There ought to be a quite different and better relationship with the [psychiatric institutions outside the prison system]. . . . And the same holds for the institution for drug addicts and for all of the institutions for alcoholics. . . . They try to get rid of their most difficult patients, and then they [send them to us]. . . . And the same thing holds for institutions [treating emotionally disturbed juveniles] ; those who have committed criminal acts do not benefit from what [such institutions] can offer. I have tried to get a couple of inmates transferred to X, but [it's been very difficult] .

The psychiatrist working in *Maximum Security*, who seemed to rank between the two others in terms of informal and personal communication, also seemed to occupy an intermediate position with regard to satisfaction.

View of communication with other organizations

The psychiatrists are clearly non-specialists in regard to communication with the Prison Bureau.

Both of the psychiatrists in *Medium Security* were deeply concerned over their lack of direct communication with the Bureau. The terms "distant control" and "decisions purely based on documents" were again used, and with very great vehemence. The psychiatrist with long tenure in the institution had been fighting a long and arduous battle against the Prison Bureau since he entered the system. He had waged his battle on various grounds, and with various methods. He felt that the Bureau made too many decisions, wrong decisions, and that its members were totally uncommunicative in relation to the treatment staff. He said so whenever he had a chance: in the institution, at penological meetings, and at criminological seminars. In the latter settings, where Bureau people at times are present, explosive encounters occurred. Obviously, the psychiatrist was not a popular man in Bureau circles. The other psychiatrist in the treatment-oriented institution largely followed his superior's example. In our interview he asked me to use four red lines in underlining his negative statements concerning communication with the Bureau. He expressed the same view openly in relation to staff members. Like the chief psychiatrist and the minister in the institution, this psychiatrist became agitated when talking about the lack of communication with the Bureau, though he did express his views with less vehemence and resilience when talking to other staff members. (Note again the contrasting view of the governor as specialist.)

The psychiatrist in *Maximum Security* deviated somewhat from the picture given above. He did not feel as cut off from the center of the prison system. When I interviewed him, he claimed that he did get some of the information he needed, thus suggesting, in line with one of the social workers in the institution, a fair amount of indirect communication through the governor. I had known the psychiatrist in question for six years, and observed him in action in *Medium Security*. I therefore have good reason to believe he was sincere, and not just giving a normative line. But it should also be clearly noted that he did not appear as enthusiastic as his governor about communications with the Bureau.

The psychiatrists are also to a considerable extent non-specialists in relation to other institutions within the prison system (excepting prison hospitals). The task of communicating with other penal institutions is largely left to the governor and to the social workers. In clear contrast to the specialists themselves (see above), the psychiatrists are largely dissatisfied with communication with other penal institutions, feeling that their lack of direct access is a problem. The chief psychiatrist in *Medium Security* expressed the dissatisfaction of a non-specialist in the following words:

> No, that [communication with other prisons] is nothing I deal
> with; well, there is the prison hospital, and then we from time
> to time call the other prison doctors, but the prisons as such
> are none of our business. We thought once, the doctors I mean,
> that we might have regular meetings, but after one meeting at
> Dr. E's house it petered out, and that's too bad. We don't have
> time for it.

The psychiatrist in *Maximum Security* was more explicit, claiming that his lack of direct communication definitely hindered his work. He felt he knew too little about the inmates' behavior in other institutions, and about the treatment—if any—that they had received elsewhere. He complained that no folder with standard information followed the inmate from institution to institution. In general, he felt that there was too much hearsay knowledge floating around between institutions, and too few hard facts. (For *Maximum Security*, the conditions described here were altered after the completion of the study.)

The third psychiatrist, in *Medium Security*, was to a much larger extent satisfied with communications with other penal institutions. It turned out, however, that he had certain personal contacts with staff members in other prisons, thus in fact deviating from the role of non-specialist.

THE INSPECTORS

In background, the inspectors in the two institutions were very different. The inspector in *Medium Security* had been employed there since the institution opened. He had studied psychology, and he had been employed as a social worker for eight years prior to becoming inspector. When interviewed for the present study he had held the position of inspector for about four years. The inspector in *Maximum Security* had been promoted through the custodial ranks, from regular guard through lieutenant and captain to inspector. He had been employed in the institution for thirty-five years. However, though their backgrounds differed, their patterns and views of external communication were highly similar.

Both viewed the role of inspector as "internal," including few expectations about external communication. The inspector in *Medium Security* explained that his main direct external contacts with other organizations consisted of receiving groups of trainees from the prison school, receiving a few other groups of visitors, collaborating with an organization exhibiting works of art in occupational settings, and occasionally discussing with members of the Prison Bureau. He estimated an average of less than one external "contact" per day. In regard to communication with the Prison Bureau, the inspector explained that communication almost always goes through the governor, but that at times he would call the Bureau personally for clarification of regulations concerning personnel matters and the punishment of inmates. The inspector in *Maximum Security* told me that his main direct external organizational contact consisted of occasional communication with the criminal police (the police asking for information concerning particular inmates) and with a nearby district prison (concerning transfer of inmates), as well as very occasional reports to the Prison Bureau (concerning escapes from the institution and from furloughs). In form, the direct external communication of the two inspectors was largely personal and informal, though, as indicated, very rare. They could not be classified as specialists with regard to any organizations. Only one category of staff members has fewer external contacts: the large mass of regular guards who, in contrast to the small "cosmopolitan" elite of a penal institution, have a highly "local" orientation.

Being primarily responsible for internal matters, the two inspectors appeared to find many outside organizations irrelevant to their work. Insofar as this was the case, they could not be expected to complain about any lack of direct access to the organizations in question. Two outside organizations were, however, relevant from their point of view: other institutions within the prison system and the Prison Bureau. The inspectors received inmates from other institutions and directives concerning internal affairs from the Bureau. Characteristically, they expressed dissatisfaction with their general lack of direct communication with these organizations. (Note again the contrasting view of the specialists themselves.) More precisely, one of them complained, at least by implication, about lack of direct communication with the Bureau. The other, dissatisfied with inter-institutional communication and, by implication at least, with Bureau relations, expressed himself in the following way:

> I think *institutions* ought to have more contact with each other, and know more about how other institutions are managed. But I am not sure that this is only a question for the inspectors. It's just as much a question for the governors—[though] it's possible, of course, that they have contact without our knowing it. It's a matter of information; we lack contact. . . . It would have been useful with greater opportunities for the employees to see how others work. . . . The initiative must be taken centrally, by the Prison Bureau. I have seen how people are when they have been around this place for years: your perspective becomes limited, you get few impulses, and you don't join organizations. . . .

The other inspector expressed himself in familiar terms:

> We have to follow the sentence, and that's what's wrong. We know the people, but in the Prison Bureau they take nothing but the documents into account. But that's the way it is when you sit far away and decide things. . . . They must rely on the documents with regard to parole questions and so on [but they shouldn't with regard to internal matters]. I was terribly disappointed a few years ago: we had given some inmates ground privileges and then we received orders to take them in again, though nothing had happened at all. . . . [Not the paragraphs], but their behavior in prison should count.

This inspector essentially viewed his—and the institution's—lack of direct communication with the Prison Bureau as something which could not be improved. When I asked him whether he thought it would have been an advantage for Bureau people to have a greater degree of personal knowledge of inmates, he answered, "Yes, but that's an impossibility for them, so you can't expect that; it's just impossible." I then pressed him by asking whether it would have been a help if it had been possible, to which his reply was that, "Yeah, it would have, if it had been possible; yeah, but that's something else. It's impossible." Therefore, rather than advocating a greater degree of direct contact between the institution and the Bureau, the inspector stressed greater institutional independence as a solution. When I asked him directly whether he advocated this, he exclaimed:

> Yes, absolutely. That's my definite opinion. It's my opinion that the things I mentioned [internal organization, including ground privileges] should be up to the governor only, because the governor is an authority, and he'd never do anything without discussing it with the other staff members here. Take inmates who have committed crimes of violence. They're sentenced according to this and that paragraph, and then that bars them from being sent to the open camp. But they can be the kindest guys in the world even though they're pretty empty-headed.

The inspector here referred to the fact that by Bureau regulations inmates with more than ten or less than four months to go, or with convictions of sexual crimes or crimes of violence, cannot be transferred to a particular open camp elsewhere in the country. It should be noted that though the inspector was particularly clear about advocating independence for the institution, a similar view was in part expressed by the medical doctors and by one of the ministers.

CONCLUSIONS: OTHER STAFF MEMBERS

By way of conclusion to this chapter, mention should be made of a few other staff members. First, the senior staff members not discussed above, generally considered as the "less important" council members, did to some degree communicate directly with outside organizations. The psychologist in *Medium Security* was, at the time of the study, in the process of establishing a supervisory relationship with clinical psychologists outside the prison system. The welfare officer and the head teacher in *Maximum Security* also communicated with outside organizations, trying to bring in entertainers for leisure time activities and teachers for various educational courses. Among the lower-level, non-council members, the work superintendents in both institutions had rather extensive external relations, trying to obtain customers for prison products. In addition, the captain in *Medium Security* communicated with the criminal police (reporting the arrival of new inmates, and escapes), the Association of State Employees (concerning wages), and occasionally with the lower echelons of the Prison Bureau (reporting escapes and obtaining information concerning wage levels). All of these staff members reported that communication largely had an informal and personalized form. Several of them—and especially the work supervisors—explained that external contacts had to have this form: communication had to be informal and intimate in order for them to obtain the necessary outside cooperation. All of these staff members (and the work supervisors quite literally) felt that they were selling second-rate merchandise, and that they therefore needed "good connections."

The staff members mentioned here also seemed to feel that relations with other relevant organizations on which they did not specialize were inadequate. For example, while the head teacher in *Maximum Security* apparently found the Prison Bureau irrelevant for his occupational purposes, the others did not, and the latter largely complained about their lack of direct communication.

I turn now to the task of pointing out certain general tendencies running through the descriptive material, and to an interpretation of these tendencies.

IV

GENERALIZATIONS

AND

INTERPRETATIONS

Many years ago the German historian Leopold von Ranke formulated the task of the historian as that of depicting the past *wie es eigentlich gewesen*—"as it actually and peculiarly was." The task of the writer of history, Ranke forcefully maintained, is that of describing "what happened" in all its unique detail, in its full "thisness."

In the preceding chapter I tried to be a "historian" to Ranke's taste, describing the staff members' various communications as they "actually" seemed to be. The primary task of the present chapter is to go beyond Ranke's dictum for the historian, and to generalize and interpret. But before proceeding to generalizations and interpretations, a warning should be repeated: though I have earlier tried hard to divorce "data" from "theory," the data presented in Chapter III actually were not fully "raw." Necessarily they were presented through concepts, so that the general tendencies now to be discussed are, despite my intentions, abstractions from abstractions.

The conceptual nature of data is unavoidable and ever-present. The sociologist—like any other observer—is never able to describe "what is out there"; "reality" is always filtered through the concepts of the researcher and presented in the light of them. The importance of this should not be underestimated. It implies that a seemingly reasonable "correspondence" between "data" and "theory," which makes a report look nice and polished, may be spurious: it may to a greater or lesser extent follow from the data being molded by theory in the first place. It is our duty (an often forgotten one) as researchers to make this possibility explicit. But of course, it is also our right to report that we have tried honestly and hard to avoid the error.

A number of conclusions may now be drawn from the material presented above. Some hold for both institutions under scrutiny, while others differentiate between them. The former type will be introduced first.

INFORMAL AND PERSONALIZED
EXTERNAL COMMUNICATION

One of the most persistent themes running through the descriptive material is the participants' tendency to report informal and personalized external communication in their major areas of specialization. With a few exceptions, the staff members claimed that their direct external communications were to a large extent carried out on the spur of the moment or whenever needed, and directed toward specific individuals in outside organizations.

The staff members' reports were largely corroborated by observational material. As indicated earlier, I spent a fair amount of time living in the two institutions, participating in meetings (primarily in *Medium Security*), discussing over lunch, and just talking to people. Though I was not able to observe all staff members in continual, daily action (observations of the social workers were more detailed than of other staff members), I was able to check the interview material at strategic places. Wherever I went, I was struck by the informal and personalized nature of external communication.

I do not mean to say that external communication never followed written regulations, or that it was never impersonal. But I do mean to say that the informal and personalized aspects were so strong that the network by no means can be viewed as a purely bureaucratic structure of relations between roles.

Why the informal and personalized external communication? The most reasonable answer was actually suggested by some of the staff members: they implied that *informal and personalized relations are established and maintained because this communication form is necessary for an effective flow of communication content.*

More fully: The prison as an institution is to a considerable extent shunned by outsiders, and thus "sealed off" by the rest of society. The probable reasons for this outside aversion are twofold. First, the prison system is defined as selling a second-rate human product: inmates with deviant personality traits, allegedly untrustworthy in view of their criminal background. This second-rate product is what the prison has to offer for services from the outside. In brief, then, the bargaining position of the prison is very poor. Second, the goal of custody is rarely viewed as fully legitimate in our society. Though we wish to keep certain people behind walls, and though we assign the task of custody to a group of captors, custody is nevertheless in conflict with our fundamental ideals of democracy and freedom. The prison system is, then, a part of society that many outsiders would like to forget about; a part set aside as shameful. Even those who take part in the very process of sentencing and incarcerating inmates—the police, members of the court, the Prison Bureau, and so on—probably prefer to keep institutional life at a safe distance.[10]

The two reasons are probably related. The inability of the

prison to offer anything but a second-rate human product might be disregarded by relevant outsiders if the prison had legitimacy and prestige. In other words, outsiders might then be willing to "help the prison out" by trading with it, despite the low quality of its product. Because of the prison's basic illegitimacy, bargaining power stands only on its human product. The exchange is devastating to the prison.

When outsiders for these reasons try to keep the penal institution at a distance, staff in the penal institution feel highly dependent on services from the outside. The range of services in question is very broad. Most important perhaps are (1) detailed information concerning the inmates' background and situation outside (used for recommendations concerning release, furloughs, etc.), (2) information concerning the policies of the Prison Bureau as a decision-making body, and (3) the promise of cooperation of outside agencies, institutions and organizations (such as the Prison Bureau, half-way houses, landlords, potential employers) in the process of release of inmates.

In the situation described here, the staff members find the most effective form of obtaining vital services is in informal and personalized communication. This form, given positive direction, is the foundation of *friendship*, and by using it in their external communication the staff members enter friendship relations with outsiders. This has several consequences, one of which is that the friend outside becomes committed to his friend inside, and hence less able to withhold required services. This commitment probably increases, at least up to a point, as the friendship grows closer, a fact which is not lost on the staff member, for whom the establishment of external friendship is a strategy designed to overcome external communication barriers.

Though intended, the commitment function of the friendship form is probably not always recognized. Thus, staff members might disagree with the explanation given here, and be sincere about it, without the explanation being wrong. Men may be oriented toward given goals without being reflectively conscious of their orientation.

Note my emphasis on the penal institution rather than on organizations in its environment as the primary locus of the origin of friendships. To repeat, prison officials feel that without a continual stream of services from the outside, they would become occupationally incapacitated, whereas staff in outside organizations do not feel the reverse as strongly. [11] Note also, however, that I do not consider the prison as unique in its difficulties: other kinds of organizations—industrial, therapeutic, and so on—may, for similar reasons, also experience difficulties in obtaining information from their relevant outsiders. Therefore, the tendency to establish external friendships may be more general. Indeed, Selznick has pointed to a somewhat similar tendency from the industrial sphere, coining the term "co-optation" to cover it (Selznick 1949), and it is common sociological knowledge that official structures regularly have unofficial or informal counterparts.

But external personalized and informal communications may have unintended internal effects which have been neglected in the literature, and to which we shall shortly turn.

OBSTRUCTED INTERNAL COMMUNICATION

Two other tendencies persist through the interview material: each staff member's satisfaction with the effectiveness of his own direct external communications, and his dissatisfaction with his lack of direct access to organizations on which colleagues specialized. [12] I feel that the staff members were sincere when expressing these views. [13] Together, the two tendencies give a weird impression of boundary communications. In one office I would be told one story about communications with given organizations, and in the next an entirely different one.

From the two tendencies one might infer that direct external communication is "functionally specific," in the sense that communication content gained by the individual specialist is important only to himself, and not to his colleagues. If so, the tendencies "simply" indicate that the staff members are not required to obtain information relevant to their colleagues.

We have seen that the communication content for different specialists varies; therefore, external communication probably is to some degree functionally specific. Yet, I seriously question functional specificity as the major inference to be drawn. Non-specialist staff members often were extremely interested in obtaining exactly the information gained by the institution specialists. Information about Bureau policies, obtained by the governors, was considered highly relevant by social workers, ministers, and psychiatrists; expressions of interest and support from treatment institutions, gained by some of the psychiatrists, were considered relevant by the governors, and so on. In view of this, it seems reasonable to infer that internal communication exchange is somehow obstructed. *I infer that information reaching institutional boundaries to each staff member as a specialist (or other services reaching each specialist, and becoming a matter of information on the inside), tends not to be shared with non-specialists on the inside.*

This inference is supported by three other sets of data. First, dissatisfied non-specialists were at times not fully aware of the specialist's satisfaction. In more general terms, a lack of knowledge at times prevailed concerning the contrasting view another staff member had of a given external institutional relationship. Such unawareness of dissensus in itself suggests obstructed internal exchange of external information. Second, dissatisfied non-specialists who did show awareness of the specialists' satisfactory relationships, at times explicitly stated that the latter did not share their information with others. Third, direct observation of daily activities in the two institutions indicated obstructed sharing. The first set of data, concerning the unawareness of dissensus, was referred to in Chapter III. The latter two sets of data will be discussed together presently.

In *Medium Security*, obstructed internal communication was commented on almost every day, and quite openly even when the sociologist was present. The general feeling was that "animosity" existed between various staff members, that the staff members did not talk freely with each other, and that "the atmosphere" was not "as good as it should be." Restrictions on the flow of information were fairly apparent at staff meetings. I participated in a large number of staff meetings (partly during my prior study of the institution), and was struck by the length of time it often took for fairly simple pieces of information to reach the surface of conversation and thereby for glaring misunderstandings to be corrected. The misunderstandings in question frequently seemed to concern relations with outside organizations. External information at times seemed to be truncated so that the content of the message was distorted. At other times it seemed to be simply withheld. Two sets of observations lend support to the latter point.[14] First, a few times I knew that given staff members had received more outside information than they would volunteer at staff meetings. Second, though the staff members individually were extremely preoccupied with external communication, specific references to external organizations were rarely made in the meetings. Though issues concerning release, furloughs, and so forth were dealt with in the meetings, these matters were often discussed as if the institution existed in an imaginary organizational void.

Few staff members seemed willing to say that internal communication was unobstructed. The governor was apparently concerned about the obstructions, because he took steps to improve conditions promoting communication. He established a canteen in the basement, for example, urging all staff members to have lunch there. Though the canteen was used, several senior staff members preferred to have lunch in their offices. The governor's secretary was also worried about restricted flow of communication, and tried to act as a co-ordinating "transmitter" of information. His attempts by no means canceled out all complaints, however.

My period of observation in *Maximum Security* was much briefer, and my material therefore less extensive. However, it did reveal obstructed internal communication, though clearly consensus about it was lower. The governor felt that internal communication presented little or no problem. He saw the senior staff meetings, the informal get-togethers, and the dis-cussion meetings referred to in Chapter I as sufficient for adequate communication. He argued the adequacy of internal communication on the grounds that lower-level staff mem-bers did not restrain themselves in coming to him for infor-mation. He claimed that they actually felt too free to come, because their questions took up too much of his time, and he was considering how to introduce structural change to allevi-ate the pressure. The sociologist, however, might interpret the pressure on the governor as signifying the existence of obstacles to communication. The pressure might indicate that the governor did not automatically provide the necessary information, or that communication relationships elsewhere in the system were obstructed. In any case, several other staff members pointed directly to obstructed internal exchange of information. In considerable measure, the obstructions appeared to involve external information. The psychiatrist strongly felt that information exchange with the social work-ers was inadequate. Likewise, one of the social workers felt that informal communication was lacking not only in relation to the Prison Bureau, but also within the institution:

> We have meetings, from time to time, but there has not been a meeting in the employees' association since [I don't know when]. And people don't come to those meetings; I do because I make coffee. .... [And it's only in our office that we have coffee together at lunch-time.]

Staff members claimed that the regular discussion meetings between senior and lower-level staff members had alleviated internal communication "problems." But they also said that, of course, the difficulties had not disappeared completely.

In short, though differences between the two institutions probably exist (we shall return to them later), the inference that internal sharing of external information is obstructed seems supported by direct observational and interview material.

Since each senior staff member generally is a specialist in one external area and a non-specialist in others, the social structure of the senior staff takes on a most peculiar total form. Rather than a structure consisting of a few well-informed and powerful boundary specialists and many uninformed internal workers, we find a structure in which each participant tends to be well-informed as well as uninformed. The structure is presented in a schematic and ideal-type form in Figure 1. The arrows indicate relatively free flow of communication; dotted lines suggest that obstructions exist. Forgetting briefly our definition of organizational "boundary," it may be said that that "boundary" of the institution runs inside rather than outside the circle of senior staff members. In terms of communication the structure is essentially turned "inside out."

It should be stressed that the dotted lines only concern indirect sharing of external information, not communication originating inside the system. But it may be mentioned in passing that communication of the latter kind does seem to follow.

Now, why is internal sharing obstructed?

FIGURE 1

Senior Staff Structure
External and Internal Communication

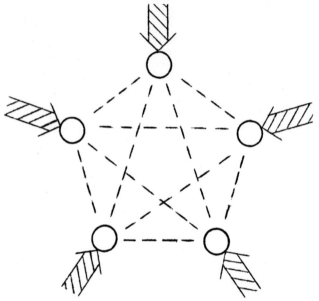

Arrows: free flow of external communication
Dotted lines: obstructed internal communication

EXTERNAL AND INTERNAL COMMUNICATION

When internal communication in complex organizations is impeded, it is commonly explained by reference to other features of the internal structure. It is the central hypothesis of this essay that inefficient internal communication of news coming from the outside may in large measure be explained by the nature of external communication.

The tragedy of communications in penal institutions is that the staff member cannot eat his cake and have it too. The more successful he is in establishing effective outside communications, the less successful he will be in creating an effective inside communication system. In more precise terms: *The informal and personal nature of external communication, absolutely essential if external information is to be procured, at the same time seriously obstructs internal sharing of information obtained outside.* As a totality the senior staff structure therefore takes on the curiously inverted form noted in Figure 1. This point needs more extended treatment.

The aura of external conspiracy

Imagine a senior staff member trying to obtain a promise of cooperation or any other kind of information from an outside organization. As emphasized above, in order to obtain what he wants, he must—since he is working against serious odds—make friends with the outsider. But by this token he also gives his external communication a "conspiratorial" slant. In a setting where formal and impersonal relations—*bureaucratic relations*—are considered ideal or at least most correct, informal and personalized relations—*friendship relations*—easily appear secret and illicit. The aura of external conspiracy probably increases with the importance of the bureaucratic ideal, so that it is particularly pronounced in relationships like that between governor and Prison Bureau.

Imagine now the same staff member as a participant in internal staff meetings. It is reasonable to expect that the aura of secrecy and unlawfulness of his external relations makes him wary of letting other staff members in on the details of his external dealings. In view of the Prison Bureau's stress on the bureaucratic ideal, we should expect that the governor is more prone than other staff members to view his external communication as going on behind the scenes, and as something which should not be revealed openly to colleagues.

Both governors interviewed for this study claimed that they were "lonely"; that there were few people in the institution to whom they could turn to discuss general questions of policy and principle. One of the governors came fairly close to saying that his loneliness was related to the aura of conspiracy attached to his friendship with Bureau members. He claimed (as quoted in Chapter III) that "these things are somewhat on the confidential side. . . . There are always some things which are . . . somewhat delicate."

Of course, the content of communication would in part be considered "delicate" by the Bureau regardless of communication form. Now, I shall argue later that even the most "delicate" content is not in itself *directly* obstructing internal sharing. But in any case, much of the content of governor-Bureau communication is not "intrinsically delicate" in the sense discussed here. I am thinking for example of the governor's various attempts to clarify correct institutional behavior. That such topics often are not communicated inside, and that they appear to be subjectively experienced as "delicate matters," therefore probably follows in part from the conspiratorial atmosphere attached to the form of external communication.

The moral commitment of external friendship

Imagine a senior staff member trying to obtain information from an external organization. Again, through friendship the outsider's freedom to withhold information is effectively restricted. However, it should be remembered that friendship is a reciprocal relationship. Therefore, though committing the outsider, the friendship also invariably commits the staff member: his freedom not to give the outsider support when it is asked for is also restricted. The staff member's external moral commitment may be expected to obstruct his internal sharing of information obtained outside. When the friend outside provides information which is prohibited according to his own organizational rules, the friend inside feels that he should not pass it on. When the friend outside reveals information that may otherwise be damaging to him, the friend inside feels similarly restricted. In short, when the outside friend provides information which to him is "intrinsically delicate" (see above), the inside friend feels morally obliged, through friendship, not to reveal it to others. In addition, when the friend outside is attacked by other staff members inside, the friend inside may feel obliged to defend the outsider. The defense may take the form of further filtering the flow of information damaging to the friend.

Here as elsewhere in this section, I am drawing speculative inferences from observations and interviews. In drawing the inferences I try, as indicated in Chapter II, to place myself in the staff member's position and to take his context of meaning into account. But it should also be noted that casual evidence from interviews does suggest that external moral commitment may obstruct internal sharing. Several staff members at least intimated that they felt obliged to protect their outside connection. One governor's assistant was quite explicit about it:

> I try as much as possible to inform the others [i.e., the other staff members] about telephone calls that come in to our office . . . Now, there is lots of contact with the Prison Bureau by telephone. [*Interviewer:* Do you tell the others about the latter calls?] At times [smiling slightly] ; my policy in that respect is that I always keep the governor informed about such calls, and then I leave it up to him whether he wants the others to know. And we can't always tell the others about our telephone calls with the Bureau. For example, when we inquire about cases which have been a long while in the Bureau, the others here get even more irritated with the Bureau because they often don't take our inquiries into account. And we [i.e., the governor's office] have to defend the Bureau a little, and be a little diplomatic. (Partly paraphrased from notes taken after the interview; the last sentence verbatim.)

The governor (in a separate interview) followed up by saying:

> I feel I have to be loyal to the Prison Bureau. I can swear to myself, but I can't let my displeasure get outside this office.

Of course, a governor's "loyalty" to the Prison Bureau does not necessarily stem from friendship relations. It may also follow from his direct occupational subordination to the Bureau. Admittedly, I have no way of controlling for this possibility. But at any rate direct occupational subordination cannot play a determining role in the external relations of other staff members, who are not employed by their external partners.

External loyalties may follow from previous employments in the organizations in question. It should be noted that one of the governors interviewed for this study had previously been employed in the Prison Bureau. So had the assistant governor in the same institution. Several other staff members had also been employed in their respective external organizations, and the psychiatrists' satisfaction with their direct external communications varied with number of years since hospital employment (see Chapter III). However, it seems more likely that friendship relations rather than previous occupational subordination as such are operating: the external organizations in question were rarely referred to as previous employers, but frequently as containing old (and useful) friends, with whom relations ought to be kept up. This, of course, is directly in line with our main argument that friendships are maintained rather than established.

The strategic significance of friendship

Imagine again a senior staff member involved in a friendship with a member of another organization. Because of the usefulness of the relationship, the inside friend may simply find it unwise to pass on information considered "intrinsically delicate" by the outsider. If the outside friend found out, the friendship might deteriorate and become less helpful. The friendship is strategically too significant for the insider to take this chance.

To be sure, from time to time a friend inside might try to

help a colleague by eliciting information specifically relevant to the latter. However, the friend inside would not be in a position to do this on a grand scale. Though it is generally recognized that friendly relations may be used for furthering the interests of third parties, and though this is often viewed as a major function of friendships in "politics," I suggest that friendships maintain their usefulness only insofar as they are employed critically and without endangering the friend. In a sense, then, the efficiency of a friendship contains its own limitation. As one of the half-way house superintendents quoted in Chapter III put it: "When you have good connections, you have to be careful and not abuse them."

The fleeting character of friendship

The psychiatrist in the maximum security prison once stated:

> You have probably discovered that in the social workers' office there is a good deal of difficulty. . . . I have tried to make them keep a diary for each inmate, but it just does not work. . . . And I have tried to make them write something down about these contacts they have, but they just have these personal contacts, and telephone calls. So this is a real difficulty. (Paraphrased from notes taken after the interview.)[15]

When I asked the psychiatrist whether he felt that informal and personal communication "sort of slips through your fingers" and therefore is difficult to convey to others outside the friendship, he answered that this was exactly what he had meant to say.

Common-sense knowledge of social relations indicates that the psychiatrist had touched on an extremely important problem in communication. I suggest that communication between friends has a "fleeting character" in the sense of being, more than other relationships, based on idiosyncratic symbols, expressive movements, and tacit assumptions. I further suggest that these three components obstruct internal

sharing of information gained in friendship-like external relationships.

1. *Idiosyncratic symbols.* Communication contains much
more than an exchange of generally-used symbols. In the
course of the development of a communication relationship,
a number of gestures which are idiosyncratic or peculiar to
the relationship also become significant symbols. As indicated already, idiosyncratic symbols are probably more frequent in friendships than in other relationships. Thus, specific bodily gestures such as movements of hands and subtle
facial expressions, peculiarities in tone of voice, and non-
standard figures of speech may all appear unimportant or
meaningless to a stranger while significant and fairly under-
standable to the friend with whom they are used. Idiosyncratic symbols in external friendships probably deter the
sharing of information inside the institution in the following
ways. First, the staff member is likely to find it difficult to
convey his interpretation of all of the particularized idiosyncratic symbols to uninitiated outsiders, so that the information which is passed on is generally truncated. Second, it is
tempting and easy to filter out specific idiosyncratic symbols: those which are likely to appear very strange or amusing
to outsiders, and those which make the staff member look
uncertain because several interpretations are possible. The
more idiosyncratic the symbols, the more difficult it is for
others to control the filtering through questioning and distant supervision of the relationship.

It might be thought that what is lost due to idiosyncratic
symbols cannot be that much or that important. However,
nuances are often strategic to organizational decision-makers.
The fact that a parole agent outside has some very subtly
stated doubts about the release of an inmate may be considered very important by others. But because his doubts are
so subtly stated, they are easily truncated or selectively filtered when passed on to others.

2. *Expressive movements.* I have stressed the importance of symbols in communication. Symbols may be defined as gestures intended to convey an underlying meaning. "Intention" here refers to an ability to control gestures, so that they are transmitted only (or primarily) when they are thought to be appropriate. However, not all gestures expressing meaning are intentional in nature. Blushing and involuntary jerks of hands, legs, or head constitute particularly clearcut examples of unintended gestures, but there are obviously numerous others. In contrast to symbols, more or less unintended gestures expressing a meaning may, with Shibutani, be referred to as "expressive movements" (Shibutani 1961, Chapter 5).

The actor may or may not be reflectively conscious of the meaning that an expressive movement stands for. In any event, the movement may be perceived by a receiver. If so, the receiver will generally interpret it, trying to grasp the meaning it stands for. The receiver may or may not be reflectively conscious of his perception and interpretation of an expressive movement.

Though there are wide individual variations, in general expressive movements are probably more frequent in interaction among friends than in bureaucratized relationships. The personal and informal nature of friendship gives a larger number of openings for expressive movements. In fact, the impersonal and formal character of bureaucracy is probably intended to reduce the number and significance of unintended, presumably "irrational," gestures.

The frequency of expressive movements in friendships may under some circumstances enhance the exchange of information. This may be part of the reason why informal communication in complex organizations is so often more efficient than communication following formal lines of authority and power. At the same time, reliance on expressive movements may make it difficult to share the information gained with a third party who is not a participant in the friendship. For instance, a senior staff member may find it hard to pass on to colleagues information that is based on the expressive movements of a close external friendship. Expressive movements, as indicated above, are at times only unconsciously interpreted. Furthermore, even when consciously interpreted, they are extremely difficult to "put your finger on": it is hard to present them as clear-cut or explicit evidence for an interpretation. For both reasons, information probably tends to be truncated when passed on to others.

What is lost on the way to other staff members may in considerable measure comprise subtle details. Again, however, subtle nuances may be of vital importance to organizational decision-makers.

3. *Tacit assumptions.* Idiosyncratic (as well as generally-used) symbols and expressive movements stand for underlying meanings. The relationship between gestures—whether symbolic or expressive—and the meaning they stand for is extremely complex. Especially important is the fact that meaning is never fully conveyed through gestures. Communication always involves tacit assumptions concerning the precise interpretation of symbols and movements. In other words, something must always be taken for granted; if we were required to express everything, the exchange would never end.

Four sets of assumptions may be mentioned by way of example. First, the sender of a message makes assumptions about how the receiver will receive the gesture. Second, the receiver makes assumptions about the underlying meaning of the sender's gesture. Third, the sender makes assumptions about how the receiver will perceive the sender's assumptions. Finally, the receiver makes assumptions about how the sender will perceive the receiver's assumptions. Keeping in mind that both (all) parties to a communication relationship are senders as well as receivers, these assumptions alone leave us with a complex network of unstated surmises.

The assumptions we make in everyday life are not always correct. Incorrect assumptions about others, including assumptions about the assumptions of others, may produce lack of mutual understanding. The point is that assumptions are not tested out. The thought of testing them out does not come to mind precisely because they *are* "taken for granted" (see Garfinkel 1967). Insofar as the assumptions are incorrect, "misunderstandings" persist. On the other hand, often the assumptions we make in communication are roughly correct. Speaking the same language, being members of the same general culture, and perhaps being members of the same organization or set of organizations, we are often able to infer how others perceive our symbols and expressive movements, what others intend to convey through their symbols, and so on. In other words, a large store of common background expectancies or interpretive procedures (Cicourel, forthcoming) often makes for reasonably correct assumptions about others.

Though assumptions are made in all relationships involving communication, it seems reasonable to expect the number of significant and persistent assumptions to increase as we move from bureaucratic structures toward close friendships. The formalized character of communication in bureaucracy is specifically intended to minimize assumptions, and to make communication as explicit as possible.

If a particularly large number of significant and persistent assumptions exists in close friendship relationships, we have probably identified another source of deterrence against further inside sharing of information obtained outside. First, if any assumptions made in the external friendship are wrong, any correct information that was obtained is easily interfered with during the inside process of sharing. Second, even if the external assumptions are essentially correct—which they probably are for most cases, since external friendships tend to be so functional for external communication—further sharing is difficult. A staff member who has established informal and personal relations with an outsider is not likely to manage the clarification of assumptions to others inside. The general friendship-like nature of external communication therefore is likely to truncate the information which is passed on, so that other staff members are left with a frustrating feeling of not knowing what is going on in the outside organization in question.

An implication of this analysis, alluded to earlier, should now be made explicit. I am suggesting that the friendship form of external communication rather than the particular content transmitted from the outside is the directly obstructing force on internal sharing.

In greater detail: (1) If it had been provided as a matter of course through regular channels, much of the content communicated from the outside would hardly have been considered "delicate" by anyone involved. Rather, it would have been considered more or less as neutral, and as easily communicable to third parties. But the aura of external conspiracy makes the middleman *define* intrinsically neutral content as illegitimate, and thereby as uncommunicable to others inside. (2) To be sure, some of the content communicated from outside friends would have been defined as "delicate" by the latter regardless of communication form; i.e., even if it had been obtainable through the most formal and impersonal of relationships. However, even here it is generally not the content as such that directly prevents the middleman from sharing it inside. Content of this kind may certainly have a bearing on internal sharing, but its bearing is likely to be indirect: *it makes a friendship form necessary externally, which in turn obstructs internal sharing.*

More fully: From everyday experience we know that "delicate" information obtained through casual acquaintance or fully bureaucratic relations has little binding effect on us, at least if it is not expressly defined as privileged communication.[16] Rather, (a) the moral commitment of friendship, necessary to procure the information, makes the inside friend feel that he should not pass on information damaging to the outside friend. Furthermore, (b) the strategic significance of friendship, important in a setting where information exchange is not at all automatic, makes the inside friend find it unwise to pass on such information. (3) In addition, the fleeting character of friendship makes further inside sharing difficult regardless of content. In connection with the fleeting character of friendship, I am, however, assuming a certain complexity of communication content. Very simple pieces of information would probably remain unaffected by idiosyncratic symbols, etc.

In formal terms, my view implies that I expect smaller differences in obstruction if the friendship form is held constant and content from the outside is varied, than if form is varied and content held constant. It should be noted, however, that I have only considered two major types of content from the outside: "intrinsically neutral" and "intrinsically delicate" content. I have not considered content that is "intrinsically favorable": information which adds in a positive way to the image of the outside friend. It is possible that such content may be enhanced rather than obstructed through a friendship relationship, though even here the fleeting character of friendship should have some obstructing effect. But in any case, "intrinsically favorable" information seemed far less frequent than the other two types of content: generally, the information needed by prison staff members was often secret and at best neutral.

It may be asked, of course, what kind of information the staff member sends *out* to his friend. If information going out contained institutional secrets, this might in itself obstruct internal sharing of information received. However, information sent out rarely seemed to contain very deep institutional secrets. Largely, staff members did not appear disloyal to their colleagues when providing information to outside contacts. [17] Part of the reason is probably that outsiders are not searching for institutional secrets to any great extent. As suggested earlier, though they need some institutional information, they generally feel far less dependent on the institution than the institution on them, so that the bargaining situation is off balance in the institution's disfavor. This is precisely why institution staff members have to initiate an external friendship form.

I have so far discussed the obstruction of internal communication without differentiating between its origin and maintenance. Before concluding the present section of this chapter, it should be stated explicitly that I hypothesize external friendships to be important for both.

First a few words about the *origin* of internal obstruction. I assume that senior staff members in a new institution start out either about equally willing to be "friendly" with outsiders and colleagues, or, since they are going to be with them at close quarters, emotionally more oriented toward becoming friends with colleagues. However, *as they get to know the requirements of their work, they will spend most of their time for real friendship developing outside relations.* The individual staff member will, at the outset, find little reason to expect colleagues to be unwilling communicators. After all, colleagues are supposed to constitute a functionally integrated, cooperating "team." At the same time, the staff member may realistically expect unwillingness, indifference and hostility from outsiders. If he is new to correctional work, he will soon discover the uncooperativeness of outsiders. If he comes from another correctional organization, he may bring along external goodwill, but since he knows the perspective of the outsider, he will realize that unless it is cultivated his goodwill is likely to be short-lived. In any case, concentration on external friendships will appear most clearly needed, through which restrictions on inside sharing are created.

External friendships probably also help *maintain* the internal communication obstruction. The individual senior staff member is now caught in an insoluble dilemma: with external friendships, he has something to share without being able to share it; without external friendships, he has nothing to share in the first place. As far as internal sharing goes, he is damned if he does and damned if he does not maintain friendly relations with the outsiders assigned to him. Since this is the case, *he may as well maintain his friendships: at least they provide him personally with important external information.* As a consequence, the internal communication obstruction is also kept up.

This, of course, is an ideal-type case. In practice, there are ways of circumventing the pattern I have hypothesized, so that it actually appears in more subdued form. But it should be remembered that few staff members are likely to be reflectively conscious of any dysfunctional link between external and internal communication. Furthermore, for practical reasons a number of techniques of circumvention are likely to appear unreliable. Three techniques of the latter kind may be mentioned in more detail.

In the first place, as specialists the staff members will hardly "curb" their external friendships in order to be free to offer inside colleagues information in exchange for information from them. Usually, the more successful the staff member in "curbing" his external friendships, the smaller is his stock of information exchangeable on the inside. A staff member who "curbs" his friendships will therefore reduce his potential bargaining position in relation to colleagues. Though he may feel freer to inform colleagues of what little he knows, he cannot count on his colleagues being open in return: they will still be tied to their outside friends, and will only receive limited reward for betraying them. Of course, if the staff member's colleagues also "curbed" their respective friendships, the internal bargaining balance might be restored. But the exchange that might follow would at best be far from perfect: the staff members would still be somewhat tied by their outside friends, and the pool of relevant information would be reduced. Each staff member might well end up possessing a smaller total amount of external information than before "curbing" his friendship. Consequently, it is unlikely that the staff members *en bloc* would dare to take such a course.

Secondly, as non-specialists the staff members will hardly be able to do what they postponed at the outset: develop counter-friendships with the specialists, thereby "seducing" them to share their knowledge. Since each staff member is engaged in outside friendships, all are emotionally too absorbed elsewhere to enter intensive intra-staff friendships. It should be added, however, that even if the staff members had the emotional strength to develop seductive counter-friendships while maintaining external ties, they would hardly solve their internal communication difficulty entirely. Even the strongest counter-friendship will hardly offset the effect of a colleague's initial obstructing friendship. I shall return to this point in Chapter V.

It might be thought that if the staff member found indirect external information or information originating on the inside more important than information obtainable through direct external friendships,[18] he might forfeit the latter entirely in order to be emotionally free for seductive counter-relationships. But this choice is not open to him. The individual staff member is constantly under pressure from colleagues to obtain external information, and is harshly blamed for not providing it. In view of this, internal friendships chosen at the expense of external ones would soon be arrested in their development.

Thirdly, as non-specialists the staff members will hardly

engage in cut-throat competition for direct access to organizations assigned to others. (Though the thought of competing certainly occurs to them from time to time. See statements quoted on pages 61 and 87.) For one thing, communication with particular organizations is to a large extent legitimized inside the institution by incumbency of specific roles, without which it is extremely difficult to be a successful competitor. Furthermore, the important informants in external organizations often wish to communicate only with incumbents of specific roles, and not with pretenders in other roles.

In short, though there are ways of subduing the pattern I have outlined, several important techniques are more or less closed. It seems that the only arrangement which would be certain to break the dysfunctional link between external and internal communication is a radical change in the institutional environment: a drastic and general increase in outside willingness to provide penal institutions with services, so that friendships, so detrimental to internal sharing, cease to be necessary in external relations.

I have now presented the main hypothesis of this essay. The presentation has been done in bold relief. In the remainder of this chapter, I shall introduce certain refinements.

EXTERNAL AND INTERNAL COMMUNICATION: A VICIOUS CIRCLE

Above I have suggested a particular sequence of influence. I have hypothesized that external communication form obstructs internal sharing, not that inadequate sharing "pushes" staff members into particular relations with outsiders.

With regard to the question of origin, the proposed sequence is relatively uncomplicated. It seems reasonable to assume that most staff members start out with an earnest wish to communicate with colleagues in their institution. With regard to the question of maintenance, however, the proposal is not quite as clean. It certainly seems reasonable to say, as I have done, that external friendships probably help maintain internal difficulties. But internal communication difficulties may also help maintain external friendships. Inadequate internal sharing is frustrating, not only in that it hinders efficiency, but also because it thwarts the expression of emotional needs, human warmth, and easy relations. In such a situation, it is not unreasonable to expect a staff member to stick to his outside friends. Therefore, a circle of mutual maintenance may be established.

Furthermore, internal communication difficulties may commit the staff member *continually more* to his outside friends. This may in turn make internal communication deteriorate still further. If so, the development of communications in a penal institution may constitute a spiral or vicious circle. Through progressive interaction between external friendship and inadequate internal sharing, senior staff members may be "gravitating," in terms of commitment, from the institution "center" toward the "periphery." I have few data that bear directly on this developmental hypothesis. But it is at least noteworthy that in *Medium Security,* where I was able to make observations at several points in time, internal communication seemed to deteriorate increasingly as time passed, suggesting an interaction effect. Thus, communication between the new governor and the other staff members started out as relatively open, and appeared to deteriorate at a steadily rising rate (see Chapter I). But admittedly, these data are imprecise. They may also be given alternative interpretations, some of which I shall deal with below.

INSTITUTIONAL VARIATIONS

At this juncture the reader may ask: may not a number of independent internal factors obstruct internal sharing of information from the outside? Why refer to external friendship relations when internal factors, such as ideological differences between staff groups and personality differences among the staff, may be equally or more important?

The major reason why I have referred to external relations rather than to internal factors, is that *external friendships and inadequate internal sharing were common to both of the institutions I studied, while ideological differences as well as personality constellations seemed to vary greatly.* In one institution there was a deep ideological conflict between treatment and custody staff concerning the general handling of offenders. In the other institution far less of such conflict could be observed. One institution had a particular constellation of personalities, while the other clearly had an entirely different one. In both institutions, however, the staff members were engaged in close external friendship relations as well as in internal communication difficulties. Of course, this does not prove my point: while the design of the study approaches an "experiment," a number of factors are still uncontrolled, and an unknown interaction between the factors mentioned above may be important. But it does at least lend further credibility to my hypothesis.

However, by this I do not mean to say that internal factors are entirely unimportant. My analysis suggests that external friendships constitute a *sufficient* condition for internal communication difficulty. But I doubt that they constitute a *necessary* one: even if external friendship were avoidable, internal communication difficulties could be produced and maintained by internal circumstances. Furthermore, within the framework of external friendships, institutional variations in internal circumstances may produce differences in *degree* of internal communication difficulty.

In more detail: As far as I was able to judge, external friendship relations were about as widespread and as strong in *Maximum Security* as in *Medium Security*. Yet, certain variations in *degree* of internal communication difficulty appeared to exist: it seemed to be somewhat smaller in *Maximum Security*. Some of the staff members there claimed that their indirect communications with external organizations were adequate. In addition, the staff members regularly expressed their criticism of indirect communications with less vehemence. The latter difference, which I tried to convey in some detail in Chapter III, was one of subtle nuance in the choice of words and tone of voice. Admittedly, the difference may have followed from the staff members in *Maximum Security* being less open with me because I was more of a stranger to them. It may also have followed from the development of different, idiosyncratic "cultures of expression" in the two institutions: possibly, rather different words or tones of voice were intended to convey the same meaning. It may even have followed from peculiarities in expression among the participants in the two settings: possibly, the individuals employed in *Maximum Security* just "happened" to be more subdued in expressing dissatisfaction than those employed in *Medium Security*. However, it seems at least equally likely that the difference in statements and opinions reflects a certain variation in degree of internal obstruction. Below I shall work on the assumption that it does. Such a variation in degree may best be explained by reference to certain internal factors and arrangements.[19]

As I got to know the two institutions, I was increasingly struck by a strong variation in degree of ideological conflict between staff groups. Open confrontation between contradictory sets of ideals concerning the treatment of offenders was clearly more forceful in *Medium Security*. As indicated in Chapter I, the conflict consisted of a cleavage between a "treatment" and a "custodial" approach to inmates. It probably emerged in this institution because the "treatment view" had legitimacy there: this was officially recognized as a treatment-oriented facility. The conflict has been described in detail in a number of earlier prison studies. The point to be stressed is that its strength in *Medium Security* may help explain the difference in degree of difficulty in internal sharing of information obtained outside. When parties representing different ideologies are in marked disagreement, information obtained outside probably tends to be generally truncated or selectively filtered when shared with others inside. This is particularly likely to be the case if external information is gained through friendship relations and not through bureaucratic relations. When external information is obtained through casual, informal and personal relationships, so that it is difficult for others to control, some room is probably left for the individual staff member to share or withhold information according to his personal desires. *This room can hardly offset the major obstructing effect of friendship with an unwilling outside source,* but it should not be entirely forgotten. Sharp ideological cleavage probably increases the staff member's desire to use it to withhold information from opposing colleagues, resulting in even less adequate sharing in the treatment-oriented institution.

I suggest, however, that this explanation brings us only part way. During my stay in the two institutions, I was also forcefully struck by a variation between them in the "personal style" of the particular individuals involved. By "personal style" is meant an individual's idiosyncratic expression of intent and meaning—his peculiar mode of relating to his environment. Sociologists generally do not consider personal style central to their discipline. I have not, however, been able to "abstract away" personal style any more than ideological cleavage, and submit that the former may be just as important in producing a difference in degree of internal communication difficulty. Admittedly, what I have to say about personal style is sketchy and impressionistic. I rely on my own subjective and intuitive understanding of the individuals involved. But it may at least have some illustrative value.

The chief psychiatrist in *Medium Security* was adamant and outspoken. His habit was to insist on his point, or cut off the discussion if he saw that he would not carry the day. At the same time, though the governor in the institution was always genuinely willing and glad to see other staff members, there was something rather "closed" about the door to his office. One did not just knock and walk in; one waited, hesitated and asked the secretary in a slightly subdued voice if the governor was very busy. This constellation of personal styles—an uncompromising chief psychiatrist and a somewhat isolated governor—probably made the internal sharing of information obtained outside unusually restricted. Again, personal styles are probably influential when external information is gained through friendships rather than through bureaucratic relations. When two essentially uncommunicative individuals are involved, the room for choice that external friendships leave is probably used for withholding rather than for sharing.

In *Maximum Security,* on the other hand, the constellation of personal styles was quite different. The chief psychiatrist there, a person with a dynamic approach to psychiatry, preferred to "get something done" by "cooperating" with the governor and the Prison Bureau rather than insisting on ideal therapeutic principles. At the same time, the governor seemed to have relatively little difficulty in communicating with people. In short, the constellation of personal styles in *Maximum Security* was such that the room left for choice was probably more often used for sharing information with colleagues.

It should be added that the institutional difference in personal styles did not simply follow the difference in ideological conflict (or any other internal arrangement): as I got to know the staff members, it became clear that they behaved with essentially the same styles outside the institutional context. The psychiatrist in *Medium Security* was equally adamant when arguing with local authorities about the construction of a new road going by the institution. The psychiatrist in *Maximum Security* showed the same communicative approach when he earlier worked as an assistant (and thereby less influential) psychiatrist in *Medium Security*. The two governors showed their respective patterns clearly when talking with me at social occasions.

Similarly, the difference in ideological conflict was hardly just a consequence of the particular variation in personal styles: such a difference in ideological conflict has been pointed out in a number of other studies. In short, the two factors discussed here were probably independent in origin.

Though independent in origin, they may have interacted in producing the difference in degree of inadequate internal sharing. For example, in *Medium Security* the ideological conflict may have aggravated the "uncommunicativeness" of the particular individuals involved, and vice versa. If so, a complex set of interactions emerges between external friendship relations, internal ideological conflict, and constellations of personal styles. This statement constitutes an extension of the developmental hypothesis suggested in the preceding section of this chapter. Together, the various factors we have discussed may produce increasing institutional variations in obstructions of internal communication.

V

CONCLUSIONS:

THE ISSUE

OF AFFECTION

In this study I have hypothesized that external friendships, engaged in by the individual because they are necessary for information to be obtained, are simultaneously a sufficient condition for obstructing the individual's internal sharing. Seen in isolation from one another, friendship as functional for obtaining information and as dysfunctional for sharing it may not be news to social science. But the combination of these components in one hopeless two-edged pattern demands attention.

The pattern is hypothesized for all major senior staff members. It should be noted, however, that *it probably holds in varying degrees for them,* and that it is clearer for the governor and the social worker than for others. Furthermore, the various deterring components in friendship, discussed in Chapter IV, probably operate in different degrees for various staff members.

The pattern sheds light on the ways in which external organizational relations may shape internal affairs. The total management subsystem has a "sprawling" character: its members are torn away from each other while maintaining intensive external relations. The pattern hypothesized for the individual member explains why the subsystem acquires this particular form. Paradoxically, effective individual external relations isolate the subsystem as a whole.

But if the hypothesized pattern exists, it is likely to have organizational effects through the management subsystem to the organization as a whole. A few comments on such deeper organizational consequences are in order.

MANAGEMENT SUBSYSTEM AND TOTAL ORGANIZATION

The management subsystem of any organization may be said to perform at least four general organizational functions: (1) Planning and executing boundary maintenance. This function consists of three components: the interpretation of "imports" (information, raw materials, etc.), the internal "conversion" of imports into products (resocialized inmates, automobiles, or what not), and consequent "export" of products (release of inmates, sales, etc.).[20] (2) Control (supervision) of other organizational subsystems. (3) Service to other organizational subsystems. (4) Innovation (modification of patterns of operation). Though other subsystems also take part in the performance of these four functions, the management subsystem is ultimately responsible for them.

In many organizations these organizational functions are performed by various sub-units of the management subsystem. In the penal institution, however, boundaries between sub-units within the management are to a large extent erased as far as functional specialization goes. Though the governor is somewhat more responsible for control, and the psychiatrist perhaps more responsible for innovation, all senior staff members take some part in performing all of the four functions. This makes for a high degree of interdependence between the four functional areas: a low degree of efficiency in any one area easily reduces performance in the other three.

I have argued that senior staff members do not interpret external information adequately, thus thwarting the boundary process of import—interpretation—export. If this is the case, the other three organizational functions are probably thwarted as a consequence.

First, the control function is probably made difficult: the management is unable to pacify members of other subsystems (inmates, custody staff) with relevant information from the outside. To be sure, the inmates' (and custody staff's) constant and seething discontent with lack of information from outside ("When can I get a furlough?," "What are my chances of getting a parole?," "When will I receive word from the Prison Bureau?," "When will I receive news of my family?," "What are my chances of finding a job outside?") in part simply results from the relevant senior staff members' lack of knowledge. In part it also results from "insatiability" on the part of lower-level members: the importance of news from the outside is greatly enhanced in a system as closed as the prison. But in part the discontent probably also follows from the pattern we have discussed: from the senior staff member's inability to free himself from the external friendship form.

Second, the service function also is probably greatly impeded. Custody staff members, nursing staff, etc., are barred from receiving information for adequate role performance. Inmates are similarly barred from information they (and often other staff members) consider their inalienable right. The inmate questions posed in the preceding paragraph are oriented to information of this kind.

Third, innovation is probably impeded. Innovation in treatment techniques—the introduction of new forms of psychotherapy, group therapy, group counseling, sensitivity training—requires new behavior models. So does innovation in security measures, including changes in the system of authority. Such models must be brought in from the outside, if not physically, at least through the management subsystem as a mediating informational link. If the senior staff members are hampered in passing on information in general, the implication is that they are hampered in introducing innovation through new models.

In brief, if we are correct in saying that the management subsystem is unable to interpret "imports" from the outside, the functions of control, service, and innovation are likely to be similarly impeded. As a net result, we are faced with an organization which is restless to the point of periodic cell smash-up and individual revolt, unable to perform its elementary duties, and characterized by stagnation. This, in brief, is the structure of a prison.

The pattern I have hypothesized in this essay, and the conclusions for the total organization suggested in the above paragraphs, contradict popular views on "boundary-spanning roles" (a concept introduced in Thompson 1962). When designed for procuring services from the outside, roles linking an organization to the environment are generally viewed as unequivocally healthy for the organization as a whole. As far as communications are concerned, my data and interpretations contradict this generalization, suggesting that efficient incumbents of a boundary-spanning role may actually "impoverish" rather than "enrich" the organization as a total system.[21]

Can the boundary-spanning role in question be further circumscribed? Relying on Thompson's (1962) typology of boundary-spanning roles, the pattern I have hypothesized should be characteristic of one of several major types. In defining boundary-spanning roles, Thompson introduces two dimensions: (1) the degree to which the organization has armed its agents with standard routines for coping with non-members, and (2) the extent to which the non-member is compelled to participate in the relationship. The former dimension may ideal-typically be divided into programmed versus heuristic method, while the latter may be divided into mandatory versus optional interaction. These constructions leave Thompson with four types of boundary-spanning roles: (1) the member's method is programmed and the non-member's participation is mandatory; (2) the member's method is programmed and the non-member's participation is optional; (3) the member's method is heuristic and the non-member's participation is mandatory; (4) the member's method is heuristic and the non-member's participation optional. The friendship role developed and taken by prison staff members clearly approaches the fourth ideal type: the method is heuristic rather than programmed (i.e., it is informal), and the non-member's participation is optional rather than mandatory (so that interaction must be personalized). Thompson's first ideal type approaches our concept of bureaucratic role: it is programmed (i.e., formal) and the non-member's involvement is mandatory (i.e., interaction may be impersonal). The second and third types are mixed. Under the conditions prevailing in the social setting of the prison, we hypothesize the fourth role, however necessary externally, to be dysfunctional for the organization seen as a whole.

The last few paragraphs raise a further question: to what extent may the hypothesized pattern be expected in other social settings? In the next section, a few remarks will be made concerning the problem of further generalization. It should be noted that I shall concentrate largely on the origin rather than on the maintenance of the pattern in various social contexts.

A conceptual point should be made. In the preceding chapters I have assumed that the sentiment of *affection* is "produced" in friendships across nstitutional boundaries, and that this sentiment in turn "triggers" external communication and internal obstruction. These assumptions are based on the general view that social relations are always "anchored" in the sentiments of individuals, through which action is suggested.

Obviously, however, friendship is not the only relationship that may produce affection in the participants. In other settings, outside the penal world, other relationships may also generate such a sentiment, and thereby the communication pattern we have discussed. For example, in the family erotic love may produce affection. Below I shall generalize to all relationships that may, under different conditions, produce affection. Referring to these relationships as "affectionate relationships," I shall discuss the general conditions under which any one of them is likely to appear in our particular Janus-faced pattern.

First, the genesis of the pattern presupposes (a) that there is a communication chain consisting of three roles: an original Source of information, an Obtainer of information, and a Third Party, and (b) that the Obtainer feels more dependent on information from the Source than does the Source on information from the Obtainer. If further roles are involved, complications may arise which fall outside the present analysis (though I shall briefly refer to the possibility of extending the hypothesized pattern to longer chains, and though obtainers may, as in prison, be third parties to other third-party chains). If the Source feels equally or more dependent on the Obtainer, an affectionate relationship is not necessary for the Obtainer: the Obtainer can just as well bargain for the information he needs, or bribe the Source with return information. In other words, reliance on affection is the strategy of the weak.

Second, the genesis of the pattern presupposes (a) that the Source is initially unwilling to provide the Obtainer with information important to the latter, and (b) that the Third Party brings pressure for sharing to bear on the Obtainer. If the Source eagerly wants to provide the Obtainer with information, an affectionate relationship is not necessary for the Obtainer (and should an affectionate relationship develop for other reasons, it is unlikely to deter further sharing as greatly: several of the deterring factors discussed earlier, such as the moral commitment and strategic significance of affectionate relationships, will hardly be operating as forcefully). Furthermore, if there is no pressure for sharing from the Third Party, the issue of sharing is not raised in the first place.

Third, the genesis of the pattern presupposes (a) that the unwillingness of the Source cannot be overcome by sheer physical force or simple command, and (b) that the Obtainer cannot be pressed by the Third Party through sheer physical force or simple command. In cases where the Source can simply be coerced or ordered to talk (which are not numerous), an affectionate relationship with him is not necessary. In cases where the Obtainer can be similarly coerced or ordered to share his information (again hardly numerous), the issue of sharing is not raised.

In short, when these three sets of conditions prevail, I expect our particular pattern to appear. I conceive of these conditions as *necessary* for the pattern: take any of them away, and I shall not expect it to develop. But perhaps they are not *sufficient;* perhaps future research will add other limiting circumstances. For example, personality characteristics of the Obtainer may in part determine whether he will engage in affectionate relationships. Furthermore, within the limits imposed by the necessary and sufficient conditions, still other conditions are probably important in determining the clarity of the pattern that is found. In fact, one such "sharpening" circumstance seems to operate in the penal setting: the bureaucratic framework existing there probably provides affectionate relationships with an aura of conspiracy which is especially detrimental to further sharing. Within typically non-bureaucratic frameworks, affectionate relationships may not appear similarly conspiratorial.

Such variations in the obstruction of Obtainer-Third Party communication remind us of the fact that at times—perhaps often—some information does reach the Third Party, however truncated and limited by the Source-Obtainer attachment. Strictly speaking, our hypothesis says nothing about the Third Party's further sharing of this information with yet more parties; it only says something about the first "loosening" of information. But if the Third Party has obtained what little he knows through a counter-attachment with the Obtainer, the Third Party may in turn view this attachment as a restraint on still further sharing. The pattern I have hypothesized may thus reappear through further links in the chain. If so, we may question the general efficiency of the "grapevine." The "grapevine"—informal and personal communication running alongside official channels—is often in a simplified fashion assumed to be extremely effective. *This assumption may not hold under the conditions discussed here.* Such a variation in the effectiveness of the "grapevine" may perhaps partly explain the common sense experience we have all had in everyday life: that news of other people sometimes reaches us surprisingly fast, whereas at other times we remain ignorant for long periods of time.

Note an important assumption in this analysis: I assume that seductive counter-attachments, however strong, will never completely cancel out the effect of the original Source-Obtainer relationship. The original affectionate relationship can hardly be entirely erased from memory, and if we assume that experience in general is always somehow reflected in action, we may expect the memory of the first attachment to obstruct sharing, however minute the obstruction. If nothing else, the fleeting character of the first attachment should operate in this direction. Thus, in a chain of interlinked affectionate relationships we should, under the conditions specified above, expect a gradual thinning out of the information sent on.

The most efficient way of generalizing a hypothesis is to specify its underlying or limiting conditions. Yet specification of underlying conditions leaves us somewhat empty-handed: we feel a lack of "real social stuff." To underline the sociological importance of the hypothesized pattern, I shall conclude my attempt to generalize by referring briefly to a few settings outside the penal institution where the conditions discussed are likely to be present.

First, reference may be made to a number of other complex organizations. For example, I would expect hospital doctors, especially in administrative positions, to have experienced the pattern. I would also expect representatives of ministries and other governmental agencies to have experienced it in relation to outside political and administrative bodies. Likewise, I would expect department chairmen in many large universities to have felt it in relation to other (perhaps more inclusive) organizational units within their university.

The conditions, and the pattern, may also prevail in non-organizational settings. The mother acting as a link between child and father, trying to "understand" the child on behalf of the father, may have experienced that her very success in relation to the child prevents her from going to the father. So may the teacher mediating between child and parents. Likewise, the pattern may have been experienced by the social worker attempting to communicate the clients' perspectives to their relatives, the spy obtaining information for his home country, the sociologist procuring findings for his professional community, and by many others acting the role of Obtainer in a chain.

Furthermore, the peculiar *total* structure which seems to follow from the pattern in the penal setting may be found elsewhere: the structure where all third parties are also obtainers, so that everybody "gravitates," as if after an explosion, from their common center toward private meeting places outside the system. Perhaps the nuclear family, consisting of father, mother and child, provides the clearest example. To be sure, many reasons may be given for the disintegration of the nuclear family. But all three main parties are obtainers in relation to outside sources as well as third parties in relation to each other, and the conditions mentioned earlier often seem to hold for the individual chains. Perhaps, therefore, we are faced with a structure of the same kind. And it is not impossible that such a structure may be found in yet more settings. Perhaps, in fact, it is common enough to make us take a pessimistic view of indirect interpersonal communication in general: perhaps a substantial number of social systems—whether organizations or not—sprawl, each as if after an explosion.

Once this speculation is entertained, we may go further. If two or more "exploded" systems are directly related to each other in a network, it follows that their direct relations will consist of affectively attached individuals who are, in terms of further sharing, more or less segregated from their respective systems. Such a network is presented in a schematic and ideal-type form in Figure 2. Hatched lines indicate free flow of communication; dotted lines suggest that obstructions exist. Circles suggest system boundaries. [22]

But is such a network possible within the conditions stipulated for the hypothesized pattern? I believe it is. To be sure, one of the conditions discussed above is that the given

Figure 2

A System Network

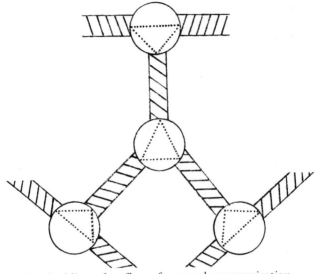

Hatched lines: free flow of external communication
Dotted lines: obstructed internal communication
Circles: formal system boundaries

Obtainer feels more dependent on his Source than does the Source on the Obtainer. But the given Obtainer's higher rank in terms of felt dependency may prevail within one "area of life" only, while his Source may rank higher in another. In other words, each party may paradoxically rank higher than the other in terms of dependence; each may be weaker than the other; each may be Obtainer as well as Source. Such a situation may be found in numerous relationships, such as between officer and inmate, officers and crew, employer and employee. If the relevant "areas of life," or criteria of dependence, are phenomenologically separate enough to subdue the idea of straightforward bargaining or exchange, and if the other conditions discussed earlier are present on both sides, representatives of different systems may seek affectionate relations with each other. They may also find sharing difficult within their respective systems. If so, systems will be related in the particular fashion suggested in Figure 2.

Though the individual is rarely conscious of such a world, this may still be part of the social "reality" within which he lives. The individual is rarely able to see far beyond his own disrupted, frustrating system. He is therefore usually unable to consider the possibility that his own disruption may be replicated "on the other side"; that as far as external information goes, he lives in a world of dispersed intersystem pairs, the participants in which cling desperately to each other because each feels dependent on the other.

One further speculation may be suggested. If networks of this kind do exist, we may have located one important source of system change. It is possible that in such a network, both participants in an intersystem pair will gradually redefine system boundaries to exclude the original system members and include their outside friend. At least this may happen if the individual feels less dependent on services provided within the old system. He may then in fact leave his old system entirely, and establish a new system with his friend.

But such a new system may in turn be vulnerable. Before the change, the affectively attached individuals were dependent on each other for services provided from their respective non-member systems—from the system of their partner. They may be similarly dependent after the change, but having redefined system boundaries, their sources will have dried up; *they will no longer be Sources to each other.* Thus, we may expect the members of the new system to stretch out once again for services from the outside. Perhaps the new system will in turn be dissolved: the services generated within it, on which it was *not* originally based, may again be less important than services from outside. The incorrigible divorcer comes to mind. A never-ending process of system change may be visualized.

Clearly, over a short time such a process of change is possible only in small systems—such as a nuclear family—whose continued existence requires that a specific individual obtain outside services. In complex systems, where specific obtainers are easily replaced by new persons, system change is unlikely in the short run. This means that the prison system will not alter dramatically in the near future.

But in the long run the prison as a system may be abandoned. System stability over time requires both external bargaining power and internal solidarity. The prison has neither: internally disrupted because of external weakness, the prison system appears vulnerable—even to the point of dissolution. To those of us who find the prison a distasteful and inefficient solution to a social problem, this possibility—however far off in time—gives hope.

Yet that hope may turn bitter. What will happen if the prison is abandoned as a solution, and the unwanted are made free? Men may then simply rediscover the utility of places set apart: organizations stripped of bargaining power, enduring an unbalanced dependence on the rest of the world, can be forced to hold society's unwanted behind their walls. In other words, places where the unwanted can be set firmly aside may be re-established under new names. The history of institutions is heavy with continuing misfortunes of change to new systems with old features.

The speculations suggested above are not researchable without modification, sharpening of concepts, and specification of research tools. But even in their present state they may be important for sociological theory and social practice. In particular, the double-edged pattern hypothesized in this essay—and the general view emanating from it—throw doubt on the pervasive effectiveness of communication through primary relations or links of intimacy. Such effectiveness has been readily assumed by sociologists. Our hypothesis suggests a need for further attention to the theory of communication in primary relationships.

APPENDIX I:
THE CORRECTIONAL SYSTEM

In this appendix I shall provide some descriptive information on aspects of the general correctional system of the Scandinavian country concerned. By way of background, a sketch will first be given of its prison system, and of some relevant aspects of its criminal law. Next, I will describe some of the most important organizations in the environment of the two institutions studied in this essay—organizations inside and outside the prison system.

When describing organizations in the environment, I shall concentrate on those performing major tasks in direct relation to the penal institutions. By this I mean that representatives of the organization in question respond to *direct* requests, decisions, etc., from the institutions, or vice versa. Organizations related to the institutions through indirect functional linkage only are little discussed here. Directly related organizations are considered because of their relevance for the staff members' direct external communications. Note, however, that a few indirectly related organizations are discussed in the main text, because staff members find the lack of direct communication with them problematical. Note also that some directly related organizations are introduced in the text rather than here.

The prison system as a whole is a state structure. (The country is not divided into separate "states" in the American sense, and "state" structure refers to a national, governmental organization.) All penal institutions are under the central administration of the Prison Bureau, located in the capital city. The Prison Bureau is headed by a Prison Director. The Prison Director has a law degree and long-term practice as an official in the Ministry of Justice. He has no institutional practice. The Bureau is divided into four divisions, each headed by a so-called Head of Division. At the time of writing, all Heads of Division had degrees in law; none had institutional practice. Within each division there are several lower ranks of executive staff members, almost all of whom have law degrees. Very few have prior institutional experience.

Each division within the Bureau has its special sphere of competence. One division is in charge of most of the questions relating to individual inmates: questions arising during incarceration, in connection with release on parole, etc. A second division is primarily in charge of personnel matters: appointments, questions concerning staff wages, questions concerning staff instructions, etc. A third deals primarily with questions relating to budgeting, accounting, the building of new institutions, maintenance, and supplies. The fourth division is, among other things, in charge of managing inmate labor and settling inmate wages, as well as dealing with matters relating to prison fare and economic compensations. Some of the Bureau's particular areas of decision-making in relation to penal institutions will be described later; suffice it here to say that decisions made by the Bureau are generally prepared by the lower ranks of executive staff members, and sent on through the higher ranks for revision and final approval.

The Prison Bureau is a part of the Ministry of Justice, and has a formal status which for many purposes is equal to that of regular "departments" within the Ministry. Counting the Prison Bureau, there are four departments in the Ministry, the other three being the Department of Administration, the Department of Police, and the Department of Legislation.

Two types of penal institutions are found for male offenders in the prison system. One is the "central institution," taking inmates from all over the country. One central institution is a general prison, taking inmates with prison sentences of over six months. The other central institutions are intended as specialized institutions for specific kinds of criminals. These institutions include one preventive-detention institution for abnormal (but not insane) offenders, two institutions of forced labor for alcoholic vagrants, and one youth prison for juvenile delinquents. In all of these institutions, incarceration is almost always for more than six months. With the exception of the institution for juvenile delinquents, the institutions are officially not called "prisons," and confinement is formally not "punishment." Confinement implies, however vaguely, that the offender is in need of some kind of resocialization other than regular imprisonment. Yet, the "treatment" which is administered is far from intensive, and inmates are reported to view their confinement as "punishment."

The other type is the "local prison," taking inmates from specific districts. The local prisons have two main sub-types. (a) "Regional prisons," located in cities and towns throughout the country. Six of these prisons may take inmates with prison sentences of up to a year and a half; the others take inmates with sentences of up to six months. (b) "Auxiliary prisons," in which terms of imprisonment up to twenty days may be served.

At the time of the study, a new administrative structure was being superimposed on the structure outlined above. The local prisons were divided into geographical "regions," each headed by a prison governor.

Maximum Security and *Medium Security* belong to the category of "central institutions." *Maximum Security* is the only regular prison among the central institutions. *Medium Security* is a specialized establishment: a preventive-detention institution. Preventive detention is a part of a more inclusive system of preventive measures for abnormal offenders, and a full understanding of the communications of senior staff members in *Medium Security* necessitates a brief description of this system.

Officially, preventive measures do not constitute punishment. They are in principle measures geared to the prevention of future criminal acts. The Penal Code specifies the various preventive measures that may be used. The offender may be (a) required or forbidden to live in specified districts, (b) subjected to supervision and obligated to report to the police or someone else, (c) forbidden to use alcohol, (d) subjected to boarding with a private person, (e) confined in a hospital or another specialized institution, (f) detained in prison. The three first measures (and perhaps also the fourth) are often considered to be milder forms of preventive measures. Detention in *Medium Security* means employment of measure (e).

In practice, preventive measures are demanded by the prosecution in cases where the defendant has a long history of crime or has committed particularly dangerous crimes. When preventive measures are demanded, a psychiatric examination is required. Almost always, two psychiatrists appear in court. They do not appear as expert witnesses for the prosecution or the defense, but are called in as expert advisers to the court, and cooperate in the presentation to the court of a report based on their examination. They are asked to place the defendant within a set of mental categories specified in the Penal Code. The most important categories are "insanity," "lack of consciousness," "mental immaturity," and "mental decline." In addition, the psychiatrists are required to specify whether they think that the defendant, owing to his mental condition, stands "in danger of repetition of criminal acts." These concepts are legal, not psychiatric, and their adequacy is arguable. "Insanity" comes closest to a psychiatric diagnosis, while "lack of consciousness" is not used at all in a regular clinical sense. It covers a state of mind where the individual is acting, but not conscious of what he is doing. "Mental immaturity" includes the various forms of mental deficiency (though very serious mental deficiency is included in the concept of insanity) and the more serious forms of so-called "constitutional psychopathy." "Mental decline" is somewhat hazily employed with respect to individuals who have earlier shown a fairly normal psychological development, but who are mentally impaired at the time of the crime. "Mental immaturity" and "mental decline" are considered as intermediate categories between full-scale mental illness and normality.

The court (in the Court of Appeals, the jury) has final authority with regard to the placement of the defendant within the set of mental categories. If the court (the jury) finds that there is "danger of repetition of criminal acts," the court may sentence the defendant to preventive measures.

A person found to be insane or to have acted without consciousness is subject to impunity, and may be subjected to preventive measures *instead of regular punishment.* Persons classified as mentally immature or declining are not subject to impunity, and may be subjected to preventive measures *in addition to regular punishment.* Among the offenders examined by psychiatrists, those classified in the latter, intermediate categories have increased explosively during the past thirty years. Today a large majority of psychiatrically examined offenders may therefore in principle be subjected to preventive measures in addition to punishment. Essentially, these offenders are viewed as sick enough to be considered dangerous risks, and yet not sick enough to be exempt from punishment. The "double-tracked" system described here is considered extremely unjust by many of the offenders who are subjected to it. It should be noted, however, that the Ministry of Justice may cancel any punishment given in connection with a sentence to preventive measures. Punishment may be canceled in part or in full.

The inmates detained in *Medium Security* are almost without exception classified as mentally immature or declining, and many of them have therefore served regular prison sentences before being detained in the preventive-detention institution. Maximum sentences to preventive measures vary in length, but they are usually of five years. A majority of detained inmates are released on milder preventive measures before their maximum sentence expires. Within the limits set by the maximum sentence, detention in the institution is therefore fairly indeterminate. The first selection of measures from the range permitted by the court is made by the Public Prosecution Authority. Later changes in measures, from milder to more severe ones as well as the reverse, are decided by the Ministry of Justice (represented by the Prison Bureau). Therefore, release on parole from *Medium Security* before the expiration of the sentence, as well as readmission to the institution, is decided by the Ministry. A decision concerning release is always made on the basis of a recommendation from the institution.

I shall now move to the most important outside organizations that perform tasks in direct relation to the two penal institutions.

The organizations in question may be roughly divided into three broad categories: "official organizations" (state and municipal organizations), "semi-official organizations," and "private organizations."

OFFICIAL ORGANIZATIONS

The most important state and municipal organizations performing tasks in direct relation to the two penal institutions are (1) the Prison Bureau and penal institutions other than the two considered in the study, (2) the Public Prosecuting Authority and the police, (3) various welfare agencies, (4) hospitals and other non-penal treatment institutions, and (5) certain non-classifiable organizations. The first two groups consist of state organizations, while the three last groups consist partly of state, partly of municipal, organizations.

The Prison Bureau and the penal institutions

The Prison Bureau was briefly described above. As indicated in the text, institutional relations with the Prison Bureau are funneled through the governor and the secretaries in his office. The governor's office thus becomes the crucial link between an institution and the central administrative body. Either directly or as a representative of the Ministry of Justice, the Prison Bureau performs a very large number of tasks in direct relation to the two penal institutions considered here. Some of them are mentioned in more detail below.

(a) The Prison Bureau has considerable decision-making authority concerning release on parole. At the time of the study, the main regulations concerning release on parole were as follows: An inmate serving a regular prison sentence could be released on parole after having served two-thirds of his sentence (but with a minimum of four months). Decisions concerning release on parole were made by the governor, after a council discussion, for inmates who had not earlier been paroled, or who had not earlier been re-incarcerated during release on parole. The Bureau decided in all other questions of parole, for example when the inmate had previously been unsuccessfully tried on parole. The inmate's application would be considered by the prison governor and his council, who would send it on to the Bureau with the governor's recommendation and the comments of the council.

In addition, inmates who were sentenced to prison for three years or more could be released on parole after having served half of the sentence. However, such release could only be granted in cases where it seemed especially warranted, and the decision had to be made by the Prison Bureau.[23]

(b) As a representative of the Ministry of Justice, the Bureau decides in questions concerning changes in preventive measures, including transfer from *Medium Security* to milder preventive measures. A report is sent to the Bureau when the inmate has spent a year in *Medium Security*. The report is prepared by an institution psychiatrist, who concludes with his recommendation for or against release. The council discusses the recommendation, agreeing or disagreeing with it, and the governor sends his recommendation and the comments of the council to the Ministry. Usually, conclusions from the institution council are unanimous. Further yearly reports are sent to the Ministry as a matter of routine.

Some inmates are detained in regular prisons, such as *Maximum Security*. For them the procedure is roughly similar. Inmates may apply for release before their first year is over.

(c) In many cases, the Bureau decides on furloughs for inmates. At the time of the study, the main regulations were as follows: An inmate could be granted a furlough when this was considered an expedient treatment measure ("treatment furlough") or when there were strong welfare reasons for granting it ("welfare furlough"), and if there was reason to believe that the furlough would not be abused. A "treatment furlough" could be granted by the governor provided the inmate had served at least six consecutive months of his sentence. Inmates serving regular prison sentences also had to have served half of the sentence. Similar restrictions did not exist on the governor's authority to grant "welfare furloughs." But the governor could not grant any furlough of over three days, and he could not grant a furlough if it made the inmate's total time on furlough add up to more than fifteen days (including travel time). Furthermore, if the inmate was serving a regular prison sentence, the governor could not grant a furlough if it made the inmate's total time on furlough add up to more than one-tenth of the sentence. In cases falling outside the governor's authority, furloughs could only be granted by the Prison Bureau. According to some institution staff members, the Bureau's practice of granting furloughs is too restrictive. Other staff members, however, did not agree with this view.[24]

(d) The Bureau, independently or as a representative of the Ministry of Justice, also decides on a large number of "less important" questions concerning individual inmates, such as the transfer of an inmate to another penal institution, applications from inmates to receive temporary release (which may be granted under special circumstances), prolongation of the prison sentence as a disciplinary measure (possible for a total period not exceeding three months), etc. In all of the examples mentioned here, the Bureau makes its decision in the light of a report or recommendation from the institution. In addition, a number of reports on inmates are sent to the Prison Bureau as a matter of routine.

(e) The Bureau decides on a large number of questions not having to do with individual inmates: questions concerning the budget, the prison regulations, personnel matters, etc.

The Prison Bureau may, on its own initiative or upon complaint from the inmate, change any decision made by a prison governor. The King may, on his own initiative or upon complaint, change decisions made by the Bureau, though decisions made by the Bureau upon complaint from inmates may not be appealed. Complaints from inmates are apparently rather frequent.

Though the Bureau seldom changes a governor's decisions, its authority to do so indicates in bold relief its general controlling function in relation to penal institutions.

Before leaving the prison system, it should be mentioned that other penal institutions also perform important relevant tasks in relation to the two under study. Inmates are transferred back and forth between institutions, personal belongings are at times sent along after transfer, etc.

In addition to the types of institution mentioned at the beginning of this appendix, the penal system also includes a general hospital located in the capital city.

The Public Prosecution Authority and the police

Institutional relations with the Public Prosecution Authority and the police are far less frequent than with the Prison Bureau, but important enough to warrant discussion of the organizations concerned.

The Public Prosecution Authority, whose supreme head is the State Director of Public Prosecutions, is independent of the Ministry of Justice. Under the State Director of Public Prosecutions there are twelve State Attorneys. At the time of the study, one of them served in the Bureau of the State Director, while three others had the capital city and the surrounding districts as their area of jurisdiction. The remaining eight State Attorneys were each responsible for their geographical districts elsewhere in the country. The State Attorneys as well as the State Director are all lawyers by training, appointed by the King in Council.

It is a characteristic of the system in the Scandinavian country concerned that the superior officials of the police also belong to the Public Prosecution Authority. The country is divided into a number of geographical police districts. Within each district, the police force is headed by a district commissioner of police. His higher-ranking subordinate officers are the deputy district commissioner, the assistant district commissioner, and the police superintendent. With regard to regular police tasks, these officers are subordinate to and take orders from the Department of Police in the Ministry of Justice. At the same time, however, they also belong to the Public Prosecution Authority, receiving directives from higher ranks in that system. They act as members of the

Public Prosecution Authority in matters having to do with criminal investigation, and when decisions are made concerning the opening of criminal proceedings. In short, the police are subject to a dual authority relationship.

The relations of penal institutions to the Public Prosecution Authority are strongest concerning inmates sentenced to preventive measures. As indicated already, the Public Prosecution Authority makes the first selection of preventive measures from the range determined by the court. Therefore, there is a certain amount of cooperation between staff in *Maximum Security* and the prosecuting authorities: when an inmate is to be transferred from his regular prison sentence to preventive measures, the institution gives a recommendation in writing concerning which measures they think should be used. At times, social workers from the institution also cooperate with the prosecuting authorities in setting up concrete plans for individual inmates. Furthermore, the Public Prosecution Authority decides whether a renewal of the sentence to preventive measures should be demanded (which requires a new trial). Therefore, *Medium Security* sends a so-called "final report" to the prosecuting authorities when an inmate's sentence to preventive measures is about to expire. The decision of the Public Prosecution Authority is partly based on the final report from the institution. In the institution, the final report is handled largely in the same way as the yearly report to the Prison Bureau. It is prepared by one of the psychiatrists, who gives a recommendation for or (usually) against renewal of the sentence. The institution council discusses the recommendation, agreeing or disagreeing with it, whereupon the governor drafts his final recommendation before the report is sent out. Again, the conclusions of the senior staff members are often unanimous.

From time to time, penal institutions and the police as such also perform tasks in relation to each other. Some examples may briefly be mentioned. Escapes from institutional premises and from furloughs are reported to the police as a matter of routine. Furthermore, the police are brought in to investigate any serious criminal acts committed behind the walls. In addition, the police at times ask for and receive information important to them in connection with criminal investigations in the community. They also perform temporary guard duty over hospitalized inmates or inmates on special leaves, and provide the institution staff with information about inmates. In both institutions considered here, some of the contact with the police is handled through the governor's office, though in many cases it is delegated to other staff members, such as the inspector, the captain of the guards, or the social workers.

State and municipal welfare agencies

Several organizations which may roughly be classified as "welfare agencies" perform a number of important tasks in direct relation to institutions within the prison system. Most important are probably the municipal social boards and the municipal officers of social welfare. In every municipality there is a so-called Social Board, consisting of at least five members elected by the municipal council. The Social Board has a number of duties, among others that of granting "social aid," often of a financial kind, to those who are considered to need it. The daily administration of the decisions of the Social Board is carried out by the municipal Office of Social Welfare. Expenses are partly paid by the national government. Upon application, inmates in penal institutions may for example receive financial support to pay for certain types of housing during the first weeks after release. In the institutions, relations with welfare agencies are generally handled by the social workers.

Hospitals and other treatment institutions

A number of hospitals and other treatment institutions outside the prison system, such as general and mental hospitals, institutions for alcoholics, for drug addicts, etc., perform important tasks in direct relation to our penal institutions. For example, certain types of physical examination and operation can only be performed outside the prison system; seriously disturbed inmates are at times received in outside psychiatric hospitals (upon application from the penal institution concerned); inmates are at times released on parole or on milder preventive measures to specialized institutions for the treatment of alcoholism, drug addiction, etc.

Other organizations

Finally, reference should be made to a residual category of official organizations, containing the Supervisory Board (an independent committee appointed by the Ministry of Justice—consisting of a judge, a representative of the Prosecuting Authority, and at least two others—inspecting penal institutions at irregular intervals and listening to inmate complaints), the "Ombudsman" (receiving complaints from inmates in penal institutions), taxation authorities, authorities in charge of distributing alimony, municipal hostels for vagrants, etc. Contacts with the first two organizations are handled by the governor; those with the last three are usually taken care of by the social workers. The superintendent of the central office for hostels in the capital city was interviewed for the present study.

SEMI-OFFICIAL ORGANIZATIONS

The most important organization, or set of organizations, belonging in the intermediate class of semi-official structures, is a national welfare association and its welfare offices scattered throughout the country.

The National Welfare Association is an association of local welfare offices working for the prevention of crime, especially as probation and parole agencies. The National Association has a board, which is elected by representatives from the local welfare offices. Its secretariat is located in the capital city and a Secretary General is its administrative head. The Association is, strictly speaking, a private organization, but receives a very substantial proportion of its funds from the national government. This part of its budget is prepared by the Prison Bureau. Furthermore, rules concerning its work as well as concerning various personnel questions (wages, etc.) are decided by the Prison Bureau. Its semi-official status has recently been hotly debated within the organization. Some feel that the organization ought to become a fully state-run institution, while others think that it ought to maintain its semi-detached status. The former argue that as a full-fledged state organization, its impact on the treatment of offenders would be greater and its financial situation more secure. The latter claim that as a semi-detached organization, the Association may avoid becoming over-bureaucratized and co-opted by the prison authorities. Though estimates are hard to give, the former are probably in the majority, especially in the higher ranks of the organization.

The National Welfare Association has divided the country into six large administrative districts, each with a so-called "inspector" as its head. Within each district there are a number of local welfare offices (in all, 58 in 1965). The local offices employ part-time or fulltime "welfare officers," some of whom are trained as social workers. The welfare officers have the following major tasks: they are responsible (1) for providing case reports on defendants when this is demanded by law, and (2) for supervising offenders (a) who have received conditional sentences or waived prosecution, or (b) who are released on milder preventive measures or on parole from regular prisons, the juvenile prison, or forced labor institutions.

The welfare offices supervise offenders who reside within their locality. The offices of course perform important tasks for the particular penal institutions considered in this essay. *Maximum Security* regularly asks welfare offices throughout the country to supervise released inmates, and *Medium Security* does the same for offenders living more than a certain number of kilometers from the institution. (*Medium Security's* own social workers are generally responsible for supervising inmates living close to the institution.) Institutional relations with the welfare offices are handled by the institution social workers.

For the present study, interviews were held with the Secretary General of the National Association, the inspector for one of the administrative districts, and eight employees in the welfare office of the capital city. The welfare office in the capital city, which is the largest in the country, is divided into six divisions, each with its division head. The divisions are primarily responsible for six separate tasks: (1) providing case reports for the courts or the prosecutor, (2) supervising regular male prisoners released on parole, (3) supervising male vagrants released on parole from forced labor institutions, (4) supervising male offenders on preventive measures, (5) supervising offenders on conditional sentences and parolees from the male youth prison, and (6) supervising female offenders paroled or released on preventive measures. Interviews were held with all of the six division heads, the administrative manager of the office, and the governor of a small, open institution for released inmates under the jurisdiction of the welfare office in question. Though fairly few in number, these interviews gave a wealth of information concerning communication between penal institutions and other organizations. I knew some of the informants quite well beforehand, and their answers seemed to be open and frank.

Finally, it should be stressed that a number of entirely private organizations are directly related, in terms of tasks, to the penal institutions. These include, among others, (1) religious charitable organizations, such as the Salvation Army, Inner Mission societies, and the Blue Cross (a religious organization combating alcoholism), (2) other charitable organizations, such as the Red Cross (which has been active in establishing a system of prison visitors), (3) a large number of regular commercial organizations employing released inmates and providing the institutions with work assignments, and (4) a number of organizations providing the institutions with supplies of various sorts. The charitable organizations are partly responsible for educational and entertainment programs within the walls, and partly for helping and supervising released inmates. In the penal institutions, the educational and entertainment contacts are generally handled by the minister and/or the welfare officer,[25] while the rehabilitative contacts following release are usually handled by the social workers.

Interviews were held with members of several of the charitable organizations. The branch of the Salvation Army located in the capital city has two open institutions; a farm for offenders on preventive measures, and a paper plant with dormitories for released inmates in general. The inmates are to some extent screened before they are accepted, and I interviewed the Salvation Army official primarily responsible for the screening. The Inner Mission Society in the capital city has an open institution for vagrants which also takes released inmates, and a fairly large treatment institution for alcoholics. Interviews were held with the superintendents of both institutions. The superintendent of the latter institution is a psychiatrist by training. Finally, the capital city branch of the Red Cross has a small half-way house taking less disturbed inmates from *Maximum Security,* and I interviewed its superintendent. The interrelations among the charitable organizations are interesting in themselves, but concern us only indirectly in this essay.

A few years ago an unusual organization was privately established in the Scandinavian country concerned: a reform organization operating as a pressure group and a lobby, working for intensification of treatment programs and general liberalization in penal institutions. The distinctive feature of the organization is that it has inmates as members and ex-inmates on its board, thus partly operating as a "trade union" for convicts. Similar organizations exist in the other Scandinavian countries. However, the present study was carried out before the establishment of the reform organization.

APPENDIX II:
INTERVIEW GUIDE FOR SENIOR STAFF MEMBERS IN PENAL INSTITUTIONS

Note: This interview guide only gives the major introductory questions posed for each issue. In every interview, a large number of probes were employed, and numerous additional questions were raised. At times, the wording of questions had to be changed. (Some of the questions appear more awkward and vague upon translation than in the original language.)

Though extensive notes were taken during most interviews (for details, see Chapter I), statements could rarely be taken down word for word. This should be kept in mind in the interpretation of interview excerpts in the text. Though they are usually very close to what was actually said, they are rarely verbatim. In some quotes, far-reaching reconstructions and interpretive additions have been made, and enclosed in brackets. Excerpts from notes taken from memory are always referred to as "paraphrased from notes taken after the interview."

Interviews with representatives of external organizations did not follow any standard set of questions. They were adapted to the particular informant and his organization. Therefore, no standard guide for these interviews can be reproduced.

1. As you may know, sociologists have so far primarily studied the way in which life and work appear inside the prison. But I am not (primarily) interested in issues of this kind. I am primarily interested in learning a little about the prison's various relations to *the outside*; to others who also are or will be dealing with offenders. This is an area about which sociologists know very little, and the area is important, because it concerns the place of the prison within the larger system. But before beginning to discuss this, I wonder whether first—as a kind of background—you could give me a brief description of your work as —— in the institution? (*If necessary:* I know a little about this from earlier experience, but not really enough.

2. Could you now tell me a little about the general contact between the institution and other organizations and agencies: is it extensive or is it not extensive?

3. I am particularly concerned with the question of whether the staff members in this institution, in their work, have contact in one form or another with people in agencies, institutions and organizations outside, and if so, how much contact they have. Can you tell me a little about how this is in your own case, in your own work? (*If necessary:* Do you, in your work, have contact with anyone outside the institution, and if so, how much contact do you have?)

4. Are there any other agencies or institutions or organizations that you have contact with? (*If not mentioned earlier:* What about the prison Bureau?)

5. Can you tell me a little more about the contacts and what they are about? (*If necessary:* What are the issues involved?)

6. Are these contacts part of the usual routine in your work, or do they arise more according to need?

7. To what extent are there written regulations or instructions stating that these contacts are to take place?

8. Concerning those you have (at least some) contact with, what does the contact consist of: does it consist of face-to-face meetings, telephone calls, written letters, or what? (*Usually asked for each organization mentioned by the informant.*)

9. Can you indicate roughly how often you have contact in one form or another with the various organizations we have talked about? (*Usually asked for each organization mentioned by the informant.*)

10. a. Are you usually the one who makes contact, or do the others usually contact you, or does this vary? (*Asked for each organization mentioned by the informant.*)

   b. *If the informant himself initiates any external contacts at all:* How often do you make these contacts upon decision or request from others in the institution (for example after a council meeting or a staff meeting), and how often do you establish contact on your own initiative, simply when you think the need is there? (*If at all on own initiative:* Do you ever discuss the matter with other staff members first?)

c. Concerning the contacts you have with others outside (and regardless of whether you or the outsiders establish them), to what extent do you act as a kind of "representative" or "spokesman" for the institution in general?

11. EITHER: Concerning the organizations you do have contact with: would you like to have more contact with any of them—or is the contact about right—or is there actually too much contact?

OR: You have given me the impression that even though you have these contacts, they are (in part) inadequate (rather inadequate, very inadequate). Can you tell me a little more about that? What would you have liked to communicate about?

12. EITHER: What about (all of the) agencies, etc., with which you do not have any contacts? Would you have liked to have contact with any of them?

OR: You have told me a little (a good deal) about the fact that there are agencies, etc., with which you do not have any contact, and with which you would have liked to have better communications. Can you tell me a little more about that? What would you have liked to communicate about?

13. Does the fact that you do not have any (much) contact with these organizations create difficulties for you in your work? (OR: Are there other difficulties you would like to mention?)

14. Do you think the amount of contact between the institution and the Prison Bureau is about right, or do you think it ought to be increased? What about contact with other penal institutions: do you think it is about right or do you think it ought to be increased?

15. To what extent do you feel restricted in your work by decisions made by others outside the institution, such as the Prison Bureau? (*If necessary:* Well, we have already talked a little about that, but there is perhaps something you would like to add.)

16. a. Can you by way of conclusion tell me a little about the positions you have held earlier, especially in places other than this institution?

b. To what extent do you find your experience in these positions useful in your present work?

c. How long have you worked in this particular institution? Have you had other positions here?

d. One final question: Do you think that people in other agencies and institutions and so on have an adequate understanding of what life and work are like in a penal institution, or do they have an inadequate understanding, or how is it?

NOTES

1. Sykes also relied on a functional theory to explain the maintenance of the culture over time. It might be said that Sykes blurred the distinction between *origin* and *maintenance* of the culture. Of course, while the question of origin cannot be answered by referring to socialization, the question of maintenance may be answered in this way.

2. They were of course also concerned with a number of other issues. So, indeed, was Sykes himself. I am here only trying to give the barest outline of the history of prison research. A few discussions of external relations did appear during the years immediately following Sykes' study, such as Grosser 1960; Ohlin 1960; Morris and Morris 1963, Chapter 13. However, the studies in question were definitely exceptions to the rule. Furthermore, they were partly of a brief and general nature only.

3. Note that other studies have shown results more in line with Etzioni's hypothesis (Street 1965, Berk 1966). However, Cline's study involves a far larger number (and probably better sampling) of institutions.

4. Measuring "importance" as indicated here is actually in itself problematical. Strictly speaking, the unit of counting should be clearly defined, and this cannot be done in a study of the kind reported here. Our analysis of staff members as communication specialists must necessarily be impressionistic.

5. Note that very little contact with the courts is required by regulation.

6. "Preventive measures" refers to security measures over the above the regular prison sentence to which abnormal inmates may be sentenced. *Medium Security* is a preventive detention institution. For details, see Appendix I.

7. In addition, of course, to many months of association with the social workers in *Medium Security* during my earlier study.

8. Of course, not all inmates are released to half-way houses. Many are provided regular lodgings, or room and board with private individuals.

9. To repeat, *Medium Security* is a preventive detention institution, taking abnormal inmates sentenced to preventive detention. See footnote 6, and Appendix I.

10. Impressionistic evidence even suggests that staff in the individual penal institution in some measure want to shut out the tragedy of other penal establishments: staff members behave and talk as if trying to say that they regard their own every-day moral responsibility as more than enough.

11. In fact, staff in the two particular institutions studied here even seemed to feel more dependent on services from *other penal institutions* than vice versa. The two are particularly important so-called "central" institutions (see Appendix I), which means that they accumulate large proportions of persistent recidivists who have previously served sentences in short-term prisons. The short-term prisons themselves, however, probably do not accumulate as large proportions of inmates with previous sentences, and are therefore relatively independent of services and information from other institutions.

12. Note the existence of some exceptions to these themes. For details, see Chapter III.

13. Admittedly, the staff members may *unknowingly* have been oriented toward presenting their own communications in a more advantageous light than their feelings warranted. In other words, they may have been sincere in falsifying.

14. Note that the data in question are very impressionistic.

15. After the completion of the study, the conditions described here were changed. The social workers in the institution in question are now keeping a diary for each inmate.

16. Note that outsiders can rarely expressly define relevant information as privileged in the sense of being unsharable with other senior staff members in the institution.

17. Possible exceptions are the governors' informal attempts to make the Prison Bureau follow their personal recommendations (see interview excerpt on p. 43). However, such occurrences are far too rare to explain the strong tendency toward internal difficulty.

18. This may often be the case. Though I assume that the staff member always views external information obtained directly as important to himself—if nothing else because colleagues ask for it—I am not assuming that he necessarily views other kinds of information as any less important.

19. So-called internal factors may originate outside and be brought into the institution, but they are "internal" in the sense of being observable, at the time of the study, within the physical confines of the institution.

20. The more general terminology, of course, is that of input/throughput/output.

21. A similar point is implied by Katz and Kahn in their discussion of "information overload"—communication input greater than the organization can handle. Information overload may lead to responses which are dysfunctional for internal relations (Katz and Kahn 1966, pp. 229-36).

22. For our definition of "organizational boundary," which is one kind of "system boundary," see Chapter I. Further research along the lines suggested in the text would require a sharp definition of the inclusive concept of "system boundary."

23. After the completion of this study, regulations concerning release on parole were changed, giving the governor and the institution greater authority in the matter. Any inmate serving a regular prison sentence may now be released on parole after he has served half of his sentence (but a minimum of four months). The final decision is now normally made by the governor (after a council discussion) for all inmates who have served two-thirds of their prison sentence. The

Bureau decides when the inmate has served less than two-thirds. In cases where it seems particularly warranted, inmates who are sentenced to life imprisonment may be released on parole after having served a minimum of twelve years. The decision is made by the Prison Bureau. This rule was also in force at the time of the study.

24. After the completion of this study, some regulations extending the governor's authority to grant furloughs were introduced. A "treatment furlough" may still only be granted by the governor provided the inmate has served six consecutive months of his sentence. But the additional obligation of having served half of the sentence has been changed to a minimum of one-third. Furthermore, the limitation of fifteen days total time on furlough, travel time included, has now been raised to nine days per year, travel time excluded. The other restrictions described in the text are still in force.

25. Welfare officers exist in only a few institutions. They are not comparable to the welfare officers in the National Welfare Association. They are regular prison officers who have taken on the task of arranging entertainment programs.

REFERENCES

Berk, Bernard B. "Organizational Goals and Inmate Organization." *American Journal of Sociology,* vol. 71, no. 5 (1966), pp. 522-34.

Cicourel, Aaron V. "The Acquisition of Social Structure: Toward a Developmental Sociology of Language and Meaning." In *Contributions in Ethnomethodology,* edited by H. Garfinkel and H. Sacks. Bloomington: Indiana University Press, forthcoming.

Clemmer, Donald. *The Prison Community.* New York: Holt, Rinehart and Winston, new ed., 1958.

Cline, Hugh F. "The Determinants of Normative Patterns in Correctional Institutions." In *Scandinavian Studies in Criminology, II,* edited by Nils Christie, pp. 173-84. Oslo: Oslo University Press, 1968.

Etzioni, Amitai. *A Comparative Analysis of Complex Organizations.* Glencoe: The Free Press, 1961.

Garfinkel, Harold. *Studies in Ethnomethodology.* Englewood Cliffs: Prentice-Hall, 1967.

Giallombardo, Rose. *The Society of Women.* New York: John Wiley & Sons, 1966.

Grosser, George H. "External Setting and Internal Relations of the Prison." In *Theoretical Studies in Social Organization of the Prison,* pp. 130-44. New York: Social Science Research Council, 1960.

Gustavsen, Bjorn. *Bedriftsorganisasjon—alternative modeller* [Industrial Organization—Alternative Models]. Oslo: J. G. Tanum Forlag, 1969.

Katz, Daniel, and Kahn, Robert L. *The Social Psychology of Organizations.* New York: John Wiley & Sons, 1966.

McCleery, Richard. "Communication Patterns as Bases of Systems of Authority and Power." In *Theoretical Studies in Social Organization of the Prison,* pp. 49-77. New York: Social Science Research Council, 1960.

Morris, Terence, and Morris, Pauline. *Pentonville—A Sociological Study of an English Prison.* London: Routledge & Kegan Paul, 1963.

Ohlin, Lloyd E. "Conflicting Interests in Correctional Objectives." In *Theoretical Studies in Social Organization of the Prison,* pp. 111-29. New York: Social Science Research Council, 1960.

Schutz, Alfred. *The Phenomenology of the Social World.* Evanston: Northwestern University Press, 1967 (originally published 1932).

Selznick, Philip. *TVA and the Grass Roots.* Berkeley: University of California Press, 1949.

Shibutani, Tamotsu. *Society and Personality.* Englewood Cliffs: Prentice-Hall, 1961.

Street, David. "Inmates in Custodial and Treatment Settings." *American Sociological Review,* vol. 30, no. 1 (1965), pp. 40-55.

Street, David, et al. *Organization for Treatment.* New York: The Free Press, 1966.

Sykes, Gresham M. *The Society of Captives.* Princeton: Princeton University Press, 1958.

Thompson, James D. "Organizations and Output Transactions." *American Journal of Sociology,* vol. 68, no. 3 (1962), pp. 309-24.

Thompson, James D. *Organizations in Action.* New York: McGraw Hill, 1967.

Udy, Stanley H. "Administrative Rationality, Social Setting, and Organizational Development." *American Journal of Sociology,* vol. 68, no. 3 (1962), pp. 299-308.

Yuchtman, Ephraim, and Seashore, Stanley E. "A System Resource Approach to Organizational Effectiveness." *American Sociological Review,* vol. 32, no. 6 (1967), pp. 891-903.

INDEX

National Welfare Association, 63, 72-73, 79, 149

Organizations: as closed systems, 4-6; as open systems, 4, 7-8; boundaries of, 10; theory of, 4-7, 24-27

Penal code: mental categories of, 141-42; preventive measures in, 141
Penal institutions: description of, 95-97; historical review of research, 5-7; inmate culture, 5-6; similarities with other institutions, 133-37; structure of senior staff in, 100-101
Phenomenology, 32-34
Police, 63, 146-48
Prison Bureau: description of, 13, 140; relations with penal institutions, 40, 42-48, 53, 59-61, 67, 75, 79-80, 85-86, 104-5, 143-46
Prison director, 42-44 .
Prisonization: concept of, 5; relations to adjustment, 5
Prison system, 139-43
Psychiatrists, external communication of: content and form, 82-84; general view of, 84-85; realms of specialization, 81-82; with other organizations, 85-87
Public Prosecuting Authority, 50-52; 63, 146-48

Ranke, Leopold von, 95

Schutz, Alfred, 25, 31-34
Seashore, Stanley E., 4
Selznick, Philip, 97
Shibutani, Tamotsu, 109
Simmel, Georg, 3
Social interaction theory, 4, 30-31
Social workers, external communication of: content and form, 64-78; general view of, 78-79; realms of specialization, 62-64; with other organizations, 79-80
Staff: personality and ideological differences, 118-23; structure of, 101
Status: lower-level, 50; top-level, 9; welfare officers, 74-75
Street, David, 7
Subjectivity in research, 24-25
Sykes, Gresham M., 6-7

Theoretical considerations, 20, 23-34
Thompson, James D., 4, 128-29

Udy, Stanley H., 4

Weber, Max, 23, 25, 31-33
Welfare officers: relationship with penal institutions, 72-75; relations with social workers, 71-72

Yuchtman, Ephraim, 4

DATE DUE			
DEC 1 3 '85			